# The Udâna

## DAWSONNE MELANCHTHON STRONG

*The Udâna, D. M. Strong*
*Jazzybee Verlag Jürgen Beck*
*86450 Altenmünster, Loschberg 9*
*Deutschland*

*ISBN: 9783849675660*

*www.jazzybee-verlag.de*
*admin@jazzybee-verlag.de*

*Printed by Createspace, North Charleston, SC, USA*

# CONTENTS:

# PREFACE.

The Pali Version of this small collection of stories and sentences has not, I understand, been translated into English before. Several passages, however, occur in the Cullavagga, Mahavagga and Maha Parinibbâna Suttas and have been translated in the "Sacred Books of the East."

I publish this translation, not with any pretensions to proficiency in Pali, but as a tribute of love to the memory of the noble Gotama, who, to use the striking language of Dr. Oldenberg, stands forth as the most prominent of the world's physicians that traversed India in monastic garb,--the Exalted, the Holy, the highly Illuminated One, who came into the world to show to gods and men the way out of this sorrowful prison-house of being, into the freedom of everlasting rest.

# INTRODUCTION.

The following brief summary of some points essential to a right understanding of Buddhism may prove of use to those who are not familiar with the Sacred Books of the Buddhists which have been made accessible to the Western world by translation.

1. Gotama arrived at three conclusions, sometimes called the Three Characteristics which are applicable to inanimate as well as to animate nature:

(I) That all the constituents of being are transitory.

(II) That all the constituents of being are misery.

(III) That all the elements of being are lacking in an Ego.

2. The only ideal worth striving after is the ideal of a perfect life, here and now in this present world, in Saintship.

And this ideal is to be reached by emancipation from Desire.

3. Salvation or Deliverance comes not by belief in the miraculous or by so-called supernatural agencies, but by knowledge and the keeping of the Precepts.

Man must be awake, strenuous, ardent.

The meditative life of the recluse is no more effective than the ordinary life of the wordly man, unless it is exclusively devoted to the attainment of Enlightenment.

"To commit no evil, to do good,"

"To purify the heart, this is the teaching of the Perfect One," is one of the most solemn texts in use by Buddhists.

4. Nirvâna is one of a large number of epithets used as names for the Buddhist ideal of life. It implies the "going out" in the heart of Lust, Illwill, and Dulness or Stupidity.

5. Buddhism nowhere expressly denies an Infinite First Cause. Its position in this connection is adumbrated by the saying: "If thou knowest the Uncreate, thou hast found Deliverance."

6. The trend of Buddhist Psychology may be inferred from the following passages;

"All that we are is the result of what we have thought."

"In this little fathom-long mortal frame with its thinkings and its notions, I declare, is the world."

7. The "Four Unthinkables" concerning which Gotama deprecated speculation are:

(I) The origin of matter.

(II) The abnormal powers acquired by suppression of the molecular activities of the brain.

(III) The omniscience of the Enlightened One.

(IV) The operation of Karma.

8. Speculations as to existence or non-existence after death and all discussion as to ultimate soul-problems, starting from predicates of material form, were pronounced vain and unprofitable, because "they do not conduce to progress in holiness, because they do not contribute to peace and enlightenment. What contributes to peace and enlightenment the Perfect One has taught his own; the truth of suffering, the truth of the cessation of suffering, the truth of the path that leads to the cessation of suffering."

The only continuity of identity of which we have any experience is the transition of the effects of the words, deeds and thoughts of an individual (by their embodiment in other sentient beings) to future generations.

This process forms an essential part of the doctrine of Karma and tends to make the general idea of the perpetuation of character without identity of substance appear reasonable. The influences shed by one who has not stamped out desire for existence go, by the action of Karma, to produce in others that 'clinging to existence' which obstructs the way to deliverance from embodiment.

In the case of the perfected saint, the Arahat, that particular function of Karma which produces this 'clinging to existence' ceases, because he has detached himself from all conditions good and bad. Karma in him has lost its fertilizing power and has become barren. Hence the perfected saint is said to be reborn no more.

9. In the ancient pictorial representations by Buddhist artists of the cyclic or evolutionary theory of existence, the ape is said to stand for that period of evolution when rudimentary man is becoming anthropoid, but still an unreasoning automaton.

10. There is presumptive evidence that the Buddha, in his purview of the Cosmos, included the origination and dissolution of innumerable solar-systems after a Kalpa, or almost an eternity of countless ages.

11. These are not localities, but states of woe and states of bliss.

8, Drummond Place, D. M. S. Edinburgh.

# CHAPTER I. "THE ENLIGHTENMENT."

1. Thus have I heard. On a certain occasion the Exalted One, soon after the attainment of Buddhahood, dwelt at Uruvela, on the banks of the stream Neranjara, at the foot of the tree of Enlightenment. At that time the Exalted One, after remaining in a sitting posture for seven days, experienced the joy of Emancipation.

When the seven days had come to a close, the Exalted One arose from the state of trance and in the first watch of the night, thoroughly thought out the chain of cause and effect, in direct order, thus; "If there is this (state), another (state) arises, by the arising of this (state), a (state) is produced, that is to say:

"From Ignorance spring Conformations, from Conformations springs Consciousness, from Consciousness spring Mind and Material Form, from Mind and Material Form, the six Organs of Sense, from the six Organs of Sense, Contact, from Contact, Sensations, from Sensations, Desire, from Desire, Attachment, from Attachment, Being, from Being, Birth, from Birth spring Decay, Death, Sorrow, Lamentation, Pain, Grief and Despair. Thus the whole mass of suffering originates". And the Exalted One in this connection, on that occasion, breathed forth this solemn utterance:

*"When the conditions of existence dawn upon the strenuous meditative Brahmana,*
*When he understands the nature of cause and effect,*
*Then all doubts depart."*

2. Thus have I heard. On a certain occasion the Exalted One, soon after the attainment of Buddhahood, dwelt at Uruvela on the banks of the stream Neranjara, at the foot of the tree of Enlightenment. At that time the Exalted One, after remaining in a sitting posture for seven days, experienced the joy of Emancipation.

When the seven days had come to a close, the Exalted one arose from the state of trance, and in the middle watch of the night thoroughly thought out the chain of cause and effect, in indirect order, thus: "If there is not this (state), another (state) does not arise, by the non-arising of this (state), a (state) is not produced, that is to say;

By the destruction of Ignorance, Conformations are destroyed, by the destruction of Conformations, Consciousness is destroyed, by the destruction of Consciousness, Mind and Material Form are destroyed, by the destruction of Mind and Material Form, the six Organs of Sense are destroyed, by the destruction of the six Organs of Sense, Contact is destroyed, by the destruction of Contact, Sensations are destroyed, by the destruction of Sensations, Desire is destroyed, by the destruction of Desire, Attachment is destroyed, by the destruction of Attachment, Being is destroyed, by the destruction of Being, Birth is destroyed, and by the destruction of Birth, Decay, Death, Sorrow, Lamentation, Pain, Grief and

Despair are destroyed. Thus the whole mass of suffering is brought to an end.

And the Exalted One, in this connection, on that occasion breathed forth this solemn utterance:

*"When the conditions of Existence dawn upon the strenuous, meditative Brahmana,*
*When he understands the destruction of the causes,*
*Then all doubts depart."*

3. Thus have I heard. On a certain occasion the Exalted One, soon after the attainment of Buddhahood, dwelt at Uruvela on the banks of the stream Neranjara, at the foot of the tree of Enlightenment. At that time the Exalted One, after remaining in a sitting posture for seven days, experienced the bliss of Emancipation.

When the seven days had come to a close, the Exalted One arose from the state of trance and in the last watch of the night thoroughly thought out the chain of cause and effect in both the direct and indirect orders. [Repetition of formulæ. *Transl.*]. Now by the complete destruction of Ignorance, there is cessation of Conformations. And the Exalted One in this connection, on that occasion, breathed forth this solemn utterance:

*"When the conditions of existence dawn upon the strenuos, meditative Brahmana,*
*He stands, scattering the hosts of the Tempter, as the Sun, diffusing its rays through space."*

4. Thus have I heard. On a certain occasion the Exalted One, soon after the attainment of Buddhahood, dwelt at Uruvela on the banks of the Neranjara stream, at the foot of the 'Goat-herd's' Banyan tree. At that time, the Exalted One, after remaining in a sitting posture for seven days, experienced the bliss of Emancipation. And the Exalted One at the end of the seventh day arose from the state of trance.

Now a certain Brahmana of haughty disposition went to where the Blessed One was and drawing near he saluted the Blessed One and after exchanging with him the compliments of friendship and civility, he stationed himself respectfully on one side and while thus standmg he said to the Blessed One; "What, Lord Gotama, is the standard of excellence for a Brahmana, and what is the nature of the works he should perform?

And the Blessed One in this connection, on that occasion, breathed forth this solemn utterance:

*"He who has put away evil, who is humble, free from impurity, self restrained, versed in knowledge, leading a holy life,*
*That man may be truly called a Brahmana.*
*For him there are no desires anywhere in the world."*

5. Thus have I heard. On a certain occasion, the Blessed One dwelt at Savatthi in the Jetavana, the garden of Anâtha-pindika. At that time the venerable brethren Sariputta, Mahamogallana, Mahakassapa, Mahakaccayana, Mahakotthita, Mahakappina, Mahacunda, Anuruddha,

5

Revata, Devadatta, and Ananda drew near to the Blessed One. And the Blessed One beheld from afar the venerable brethren approaching and when he saw them he called to his disciples and said; "Behold, O Bhikkhus, these venerable Brahmanas approaching, behold, O Bhikkhus these venerable Brahmanas drawing nigh."

When these words had been spoken a certain Bhikkhu, by birth a Brahmana, said to the Blessed One: "What is the standard of conduct required of a Brahmana and what is the nature of the works he should perform?"

And the Blessed One, in this connection, on that occasion, breathed forth this solemn utterance:

*"Those who walk ever mindful, who have put away evil, who have destroyed the fetters, the wise ones,*
*These verily in this world are Brahmanas."*

6. Thus have I heard. On a certain occasion the Blessed One dwelt at Râjagaha in the Bambu Grove, in Kalandika-nivâpa. At that time the venerable Mahakassapa abode in the Pipphali cave and was stricken with a sore disease. Subsequently the venerable Mahakassapa recovered from the disease and when he was restored to health, this thought occurred to him: "What if I were to enter Râjagaha in quest of alms?" Now at that time there were some 500 Devas in attendance upon the venerable Mahakassapa, who were zealously engaged in procuring alms for him. And the venerable Mahakassapa, dismissing the 500 Devas, robed himself in the forenoon and taking with him his alms bowl and tunic, entered Râjagaha for alms and went to the slums, the streets of the poor and the alleys where the weavers resided.

And the Blessed One beheld the venerable Mahakassapa wandering about in Râjagaha for alms, in the slums, in the streets of the poor and the alleys where the weavers resided.

And the Blessed One, in this connection, on that occasion, breathed forth this solemn utterance:

*"He who cherishes the forsaken and the unknown, who has subdued himself,*
*Who stands firm in the truth, who has destroyed evil, and put away sin,*
*That man I call a Brahmana."*

7. Thus have I heard. On a certain occasion the Blessed One dwelt at Pâtali, at the Ajakalâpaka monastery, in the cell of the Yakkha, Ajakalâpaka. Now at that time the Blessed One was sitting in the open air, the darkness of the night was profound, and from a cloud there fell, one by one, drops of rain. And the Yakkha, Ajakalâpaka, desirous of causing terror, trembling, and horripilation to the Blessed One, approached the Blessed One, and when he had arrived quite close to him, he uttered three piercing shrieks, crying out, "This, O Samana, is thy evil spirit." And the Blessed One, in this connection, on that occasion, breathed forth this solemn utterance:

*"When the Brahmana, in knowledge, has passed beyond the conditions of existence,*
*Him neither goblin nor fiend can terrify."*

8. Thus have I heard. On a certain occasion the Blessed One dwelt at Savatthi, in the Jetavana, the garden of Anâthapindika. At that time the venerable Sangamaji had arrived at Savatthi to see the Blessed One.

Now the old wife of the venerable Sangamaji heard that her lord, Sangamaji, had arrived at Savatthi, so taking her child with her, she went to the Jetavana.

At that time the venerable Sangamaji was sitting at the foot of a certain tree, enjoying a noonday rest. And the old wife went to where the venerable Sangamaji was, and drawing near to him, said, "This, O Samana, is thy little son, cherish thou him."

When she had thus spoken, the venerable Sangamaji remained silent. A second and a third time she said: "This, O Samana, is thy little son, cherish thou him." When she had thus spoken, the venerable Sangamaji remained silent. Then the old wife, depositing the child in the presence of the venerable Sangamaji, took her departure, saying: "This, O Samana, is thy son, cherish thou him." And the venerable Sangamaji neither looked at the child nor spoke to him. Then the old wife with the assent of the venerable Sangamaji withdrew for a short distance, and when she saw that the venerable Sangamaji neither looked at the child nor spoke to him, this thought occurred to her, "This Samana cares not for his son", and turning away, she took her son and departed.

And the Blessed One, with divine vision, clear and surpassing that of men, beheld this discomfiture of the old wife of the venerable Sangamaji.

And the Blessed One, in this connection, on that occasion, breathed forth this solemn utterance:

*"He neither rejoices at his arrival, nor grieves at his departure:*
*This Sangamaji, freed from attachment, him I call a Brahmana."*

9. Thus have I heard. On a certain occasion the Blessed One dwelt at Gayasisa, near Gaya. At that time near the Gaya there was a large concourse of ascetics, with matted hair, who, in the icy winter nights, and in the early morning cold were emerging from and plunging into the water near Gaya, anointing each other, and sacrificing with fire--thinking by such means to obtain purification.

And the Blessed One beheld these ascetics, with matted hair, emerging from and plunging into the water near Gaya, anointing each other, and sacrificing with fire, thinking by such means to obtain purification.

And the Blessed One, in this connection, on that occasion, breathed forth this solemn utterance:

*"Purification cometh not by water, though the people bathe ever so long;*
*In whom truth and religion abide, that man is pure, he is a Brahmana."*

10. Thus have I heard. On a certain occasion the Blessed One dwelt at Savatthi, in the Jetavana, the garden of Anâthapindika. At that time Bahiya Daruciriya abode at Supparika, on the seashore. He was respected, held in reverence, honoured and esteemed. He was also a recipient of the requisites of a monk, namely, robes, alms, bed and medicine in case of sickness. And this thought occurred to Bahiya Daruciriya: "Am I not, indeed, one of those who are Saints in this world, or, at least, one of those who have entered the path on the way to Saintship."

And certain Devas, former blood-relations of Bahiya Daruciriya, who were compassionate and interested in his welfare, perceived with their own minds the thought that occurred to Bahiya Daruciriya. They went to where he was, and drawing near to him, said; "You, O Bahiya are neither a Saint, nor have you entered the path which leads to Saintship. The course which you pursue is not such that thereby you will become a Saint, or enter the path which leads to Saintship. But there are, in these days, both in this world and the world of gods, saints and those who have entered the path which leads to Saintship. There is, O Bahiya, in the north country, a city called Savatthi. There, at this very time, dwells the Exalted One, that Saint, the Supreme Buddha: and that Blessed One, that Saint, teaches the doctrine of Saintship." And Bahiya incited by these Devas departed from Supparika and in the course of one night reached Savatthi, where the Exalted One dwelt, in the Jetavana, the garden of Anâthapindika. At that time a great number of mendicants were taking exercise in the open air. And Bahiya went to where the mendicants were and drawing near said to them: "Where tarries now, Reverend Sirs, the Exalted One, that Saint, the Supreme Buddha? I am longing to see the Exated One, that Saint, the Supreme Buddha."

"The Exalted One, O Bahiya, has entered the inner courts to receive alms."

And Bahiya, trembling with agitation and departing from the Jetavana beheld the Exalted One going on his rounds for alms in Savatthi--the Lord, gracious, beautiful to behold, with senses stilled and mind restrained, as one who has attained the supreme calm of self conquest, subdued and guarded. And when he beheld him, he went to where the Exalted One was and drawing near, he bowed his head in salutation at the feet of the Exalted One and said: "Teach me, O Exalted One, the doctrine; O happy One, teach me the doctrine, so that throughout the length of my days it may conduce to my happiness and welfare." When these words had been spoken the Blessed One said to Bahiya; "The time is ill-chosen, I have entered the city for alms."

A second time Bahiya Daruciriya said to the Blessed One: "It is hard, Sire, to know to which of us death will first come; whether to the Blessed One or to me; teach me the doctrine, O, Blessed One; O, Happy One,

8

teach me the doctrine, so that throughout the length of my days, it may be for my welfare and happiness."

A second time the Blessed One said to Bahiya: "The time is ill-chosen, I have entered the city for alms."

[Bahiya addresses the Blessed One a third time, as above. *Transl.*]

"Thus, O Bahiya, you should learn; of the seen, only a little is seen, of the heard only a little is heard, of the thought only a little is thought, of the known only a little is known; so, O Bahiya, it should be learnt: in as much as of the seen only a little is seen etc., [Text here corrupt and commentary deficient. *Translator*]; that is the end of suffering."

And the heart of Bahiya, by the concise exposition of the Doctrine by the Blessed One, was freed from 'attachment' and the Sins. And when the Blessed One had thus concisely admonished Bahiya, he took his departure. Now it came to pass that soon after the departure of the Blessed One, Bahiya was thrown down by a wild calf and killed. And when the Blessed One had gone his rounds for alms and finished his meal for the day, he left the city accompanied by a large retinue of Bhikkhus and beheld Bahiya Daruciriya lying dead. And he called the Bhikkhus to him and said; "Take, O Bhikkhus, the body of Bahiya, place it on a bed, bear it away and cremate it, and afterwards erect a mound over the remains--for this, O Bhikkhus, is a fellow-saint who has died."

"So be it, Sire", said the Bhikkhus in assent to the Blessed One. And they took the body of Bahiya, placed it on a bed, bore it away and cremated it and afterwards erected a mound over the remains.

And they went to where the Blessed One was and drawing near they saluted the Blessed One and sat down respectfully on one side and while thus sitting these Bhikkhus said to the Blessed One; "The body of Bahiya, Sire, has been cremated and the mound erected; whither has he gone and what will be his future state?"

"A wise man, O Bhikkhus, was Bahiya; he practised the lesser duties for the attainment of the highest state, he vexed me with no questions concerning the Doctrine. Bahiya Daruciriya, O Bhikkhus, has ceased to exist."

And the Blessed One, in this connection, on that occasion, breathed forth this solemn utterance:--

*"Where water, earth, heat, air no footing find,*
*There burns not any light, nor shines the Sun,*
*The Moon sheds not her radiant beams,*
*The home of Darkness is not there.*
*When in deep silent hours of thought*
*The holy sage to Truth attains,*
*Then is he free from joy and pain,*
*From Form and Formless worlds released."*

# CHAPTER II. MUCILINDA.

1. Thus have I heard. On a certain occasion, subsequent to his attainment of Buddhahood, the Blessed One dwelt at Uruvela, on the banks of the stream Neranjara at the foot of the Mucilinda tree.

At that time, the Blessed One, having sat in an attitude of meditation for seven days, experienced the bliss of Emancipation.

Now it came pass that a great cloud appeared, out of season, and for seven days rain fell, cold winds blew and darkness prevailed. And the Serpent King, Mucilinda, came forth from his hidden realm and winding his coils seven times around the body of the Blessed One, he formed with his serpent's hood a great canopy above the head of the Buddha, and he uttered these words to himself; "may no coldness touch the Blessed One, nor any heat, may no gadflies or gnats, or winds, or sunheat distress the Blessed One."

And the Blessed One, at the close of the seventh day arose from that state of trance and Mucilinda, the Serpent King, seeing that the sky was clear and cloudless, loosed his coils from around the body of the Blessed One and concealing his own nature, took upon him the form of a youth and stood before the Blessed One with folded hands, worshipping him. And the Blessed One, in this connection, on that occasion, breathed forth this solemn utterance:

*"How sweet the solitude of the peaceful, of him who has heard and perceived the Truth!*

*Happy to be without malice! restraintful towards all beings!*

*Happy are the passion-free! Happy he who overcomes Desire!*

*To have removed the notion 'I am', that is the supreme joy!"*

2. Thus have I heard. On a certain occasion the Blessed One dwelt at Savatthi, in the Jetavana, the garden of Anâthapindika.

At that time a great number of Bhikkhus, when they had gone their rounds and finished the midday repast, assembled and fell into their places in the State room of the monastery. And a dispute arose to this effect; "Which, O Brothers, of the two Kings, the King Magadha Seniya Bimbasâra or the King Pasenadi Kosala, is the wealthiest, the possessor of the largest property, of treasure and chariots, which is the strongest, the most powerful, the most mighty?" Such were the dispute and contention which occupied these Bhikkhus at this time.

And the Blessed One, at even tide, arose from his solitary communings and went to the State room of the monastery and when he arrived there, he sat down on the appointed seat and while thus sitting, he called the Bhikkhus to him and said; "on what subject, O Bhikkhus, have dispute and contention arisen amongst you assembled and congregated here?"

Just now, Sire, when we had gone our rounds and finished the midday repast we assembled and fell into our places in the State room of the monastery and a dispute arose to this effect; [as above. *Translator*].

That, Sire, was the subject of dispute and contention among us, when the Blessed One arrived.

"It is not fitting, O Bhikkhus, for such as you, scions of noble families, who for the sake of the faith, have abandoned your homes for the homeless state, to engage in such disputes. When you assemble, O Bhikkhus, one of these two is obligatory, religious discourse or a noble silence."

And the Blessed One, in this connection, on that occasion, breathed forth this solemn utterance:

*"Whatever of sensual pleasure there may be on earth, or in the kingdom of the gods,*
*It is not worth a sixteenth part of the joy which springs from the destruction of Desire."*

3. Thus have I heard. On a certain occasion the Blessed One dwelt at Savatthi, in the Jetavana, the garden of Anâthapindika.

At that time a number of youths, somewhere between Savatthi and the Jetavana, were attacking a snake with sticks. And the Blessed One, robing himself in the forenoon and taking with him his almsbowl and tunic, entered Savatthi to receive alms. And the Blessed One saw these youths, somewhere between Savatthi and the Jetavana, attacking a snake with sticks.

And the Blessed One, in this connection, on that occasion breathed forth this solemn utterance:

*"He was seeking his own pleasure, does injury to the living,*
*For such a one there is no happiness hereafter.*
*But he who seeking his own pleasure, injures not the living,*
*For such a one there is happiness hereafter."*

4. Thus have I heard. On a certain occasion the Blessed One dwelt at Savatthi, in the Jetavana, the garden of Anâthapindika. At that time the Blessed One was respected, reverenced, held in awe and esteemed. He was a recipient of the requisites of a monk, such as robes, alms, bed and medicine in case of sickness. The Brotherhood also was respected, reverenced, honoured, held in awe and esteemed, and received the requisites of monks such as robes, alms, bed and medicine in case of sickness.

The wandering monks, however, adherents of heretical sects were not held in honour and were not recipients of the requisites of monks.

And these wandering monks, adherents of heretical sects could not endure the honour paid to the Blessed One and the Brotherhood, and whenever they saw the disciples of the Blessed One, in the villages or the woods, they abused, reviled, annoyed and worried them, making use of vile and harsh expressions.

And a large number of disciples went to where the Blessed One was, and drawing near saluted the Blessed One and sat down respectfully apart and while thus sitting these disciples said to the Blessed One: "The Blessed One, Sire, is honoured, etc. [as above. *Transl.*]

The Brotherhood is honoured, etc. d°.

The wandering monks are not held in honor. d°.

And the Blessed One, in this connection, on that occasion, breathed forth this solemn utterance:--

*"He who in village or in grove comes in contact with ease or discomfort,*
*Should not put it to the charge of himself or others.*
*The contacts of sensation affect a man on account of his Upadhi.*
*flow can they affect him who has freed himself from Upadhi?"*

5. Thus have I heard. On a certain occasion the Blessed One dwelt at Savatthi, in the Jetavana, the garden of Anâthapindika.

At that time a certain lay disciple, by name Icchanangolaka arrived at Savatthi for the purpose of transacting some business. When this lay disciple had completed what he had to do at Savatthi, he went to where the Blessed One was, and drawing near he saluted the Blessed One and sat down respectfully apart. And the Blessed One said to the disciple as he sat there: "For a long time, O disciple, you have behaved in this manner, that is, with regard to coming here."

"For a long time, Sire, I have desired to approach and see the Blessed One, but I have been deterred by business, so I have been unable to approach and see the Blessed One."

And the Blessed One, in this connection, on that occasion, breathed forth this solemn utterance:--

*"Happy is that upright and learned one who has no possessions!*
*See how the rich man is troubled;*
*How one man is in bondage to another."*

6.--Omitted.

7. Thus have I heard. On a certain occasion, the Blessed One dwelt at Savatthi, in the Jetavana, the garden of Anâthapindika. Now, at that time, a little child, the only and dearly loved son of a certain lay disciple, died. And a number of lay disciples, with garments and hair wet (with tears) went, at inconvenient hours, to where the Blessed One was, and drawing near, they saluted the Blessed One and sat down respectfully apart. And as they thus sat apart, the Blessed One spoke to them saying: "Wherefore, O disciples, do you thus approach me at inconvenient hours, with garments and hair wet with tears?" When these words had been spoken, the lay disciple said to the Blessed One: "Sire, my only and dearly loved little son is dead, for this reason we come, at unseasonable hours, with garments and hair wet (with tears)." And the Blessed One, in this connection, on that occasion breathed forth this solemn utterance:--

*"The retinue of the gods and the unconverted,*
*Clinging to the joys and delights of form,*
*Depart into the power of the King of Death,*
*To wither and to weep.*
*But those who keep vigil by night and by day,*
*And forsake all that is loveable in form;*
*They truly dig up the root of sorrow.*
*Hard is it to overcome the temptations*
*That lead unto Death."*

8. Thus have I heard. On a certain occasion the Blessed One dwelt at Kundi in the Kunditthâna Grove. Now at that time Suppavâsa, the daughter (of the King) of Koliya, had been in travail for seven days, after remaining childless for seven years. She, stricken with acute, piercing, terrible pains, found consolation in these three reflections;

"Surely, there is the Exalted One, the supreme Buddha who preaches the Doctrine whereby such pains as these are left behind."

"Surely, there are the disciples of the Exalted One, who walk in righteousness, who have entered the path where pains like these are left behind."

"O happy, too happy Nirvâna, where pains like these will be no more!"

And Suppavâsa, the daughter (of the King) of Koliya called her husband and said; "Go, my Lord, to where the Exalted One tarries, and when you have drawn near to him, in my name bow down your head in salutation at the feet of the Exalted One, and ask if there is any slight ailment, if the Blessed One is free from bodily suffering and in vigorous health, and speak thus; "Suppavâsa, Sire, the daughter (of the King) of Koliya, bows her head in salutation at the feet of the Exalted One and asks if there is any slight ailment, if the Blessed One is free from bodily suffering, in vigorous health and in the enjoyment of life."

And say; "Suppavâsa, Sire, the daughter (of the King) of Koliya was childless for seven years and now has been in travail for seven days; she, stricken with acute, [as above] pains, finds consolation in these three reflections; [repetition as above. *Transl.*].

"Be it so;" said Koliyaputta, in assent to Suppavâsa the daughter of Koliya, and he went to where the Blessed One was and having saluted the Blessed One, he stood respectfully on one side and while thus standing he said to the Blessed One; "Suppavâsa, Sire, the daughter of Koliya bows her head. . . . [repetition as above. *Transl.*].

(And the Blessed One said); "Let it be well with Suppavâsa, the daughter of Koliya, let her bring forth in health a healthy son." (At the very moment the Blessed One spoke these words, it was well with Suppavâsa, the daughter of Koliya and she brought forth in health a healthy son).

"So be it, Sire," said Koliyaputta praising the words of the Blessed One and giving thanks. Then he arose from his seat and having saluted the Blessed One, passing round with his right side to him, he returned to his own house. And Koliyaputta saw that it was well with Suppavâsa and that she had brought forth a healthy son and when he beheld her, he thought to himself; "How marvellous, how wonderful is the great strength and mighty power of the Perfect One, that at the very moment the Blessed One spoke these words, it was well with Suppavâsa, and she brought forth in health a healthy son." And he was happy, gladdened and overjoyed.

And Suppavâsa cailed her husband and said; "Go, my Lord, to where the Blessed One is and drawing near to him, in my name bow your head in salutation at the feet of the Blessed One and say thus; "Suppavâsa, Sire, the daughter of Koliya, was childless for seven years, and for seven days she was in travail: it is now well with her, and she has brought forth in health a healthy son, she invites the Brethren to take their meals with her for seven days. May it please the Blessed One and the Brethren to take their meals with Suppavâsa the daughter of Koliya for seven days."

"Be it so," said Koliyaputta in assent to Suppavâsa and he went to where the Blessed One was and drawing near be saluted the Blessed One, and sat down respectfully apart, and while thus sitting he said to the Blessed One; "Suppavâsa, Sire, the daughter of Koliya bows her head . . . [as above. *Transl.*]. May it please the Blessed One and the Brethren to take their meals with her for seven days."

Now at that time, the Brotherhood with the Buddha at their head had been invited by a certain lay disciple to take their morrow's meal with him. And that lay disciple was the servitor of the venerable Maha Moggallana. And the Blessed One called the venerable Maha Moggallana to him and said; "Go thou, Moggalana, to where that disciple is and drawing near to him, say; "Friend, Suppavâsa, the daughter of Koliya who was childless for seven years . . . . [repetition. *Transl.*] has invited the Blessed One and the Brotherhood to take their meals with her for seven days. Permit Suppavâsa to provide these seven meals, afterwards you servitor shall provide the meal."

"Be it so, Sire," said the venerable Maha Moggalana in assent to the Blessed One and be went to where that lay disciple was and drawing near he said to him; "Suppavâsa, friend, . . . . [repetition. *Transl.*] has invited . . . . . . . [repetition. *Transl.*] . . . . . afterwards, you shall provide the meal." "If the lord Maha Moggalana will be my surety for three things, my property, my life and my faith, then let Suppavâsa the daughter of Koliya provide the seven meals, and afterwards I will provide the meal."

"For two of these things, friend, I will be your surety, for your property and your life, but you must be your own surety in respect of the faith."

14

If the Lord Maha Moggallana will be my surety for these two things, my property and my life, then let Suppavâsa provide the seven meals and afterwards I will provide the meal.

Then the venerable Maha Moggalana, having persuaded the lay disciple, went to where the Blessed One was and drawing near said to the Blessed One; "I have, Sire, persuaded the lay disciple to allow Suppavâsa to provide the seven meals and afterwards he will provide the meal."

Then Suppavâsa, the daughter of Koliya, for seven days with her own hands, made ready sweet food, both hard and soft and served it to the Brotherhood and the Buddha, as the principal guest. And she did homage to the child and to the Blessed One and the Brotherhood.

And the venerable Sariputta said to the child; "I trust, child, that you are at ease, that you have sufficient food to support life, that you do not suffer in any respect."

How, reverend Sariputta, can I be at ease, how can I be doing well, since I have been the cause of suffering to my mother for seven years?"

And Suppavâsa said to herself; "My son is conversing with the 'Captain of the Faith'." And she rejoiced exceedingly and became enraptured and was filled with joy. And the Blessed One said to Suppavâsa, the daughter of Koliya; "Suppavâsa, would you have another son such as this one?"

"I would have, Blessed One, seven other sons such as this one."

And the Blessed One, in this connection, on that occasion, breathed forth this solemn utterance:--

*"Joylessness in the guise of joy, delight in the guise of misery,*
*Pain in the guise of happiness, take possession of the thoughtless".*

9. Thus have I heard. On a certain occasion the Blessed One dwelt at Savatthi, in the Eastern Monastery, in the pavilion of Visakha Migaramata.

At that time Visakha Migaramata, desirous of obtaining some favor, importuned the King Pasenadi Kosala. The King Pasenadi Kosala did not accede to her request.

And Visakha Migaramata went, at an unseasonable hour, to where the Blessed One was and drawing near she saluted the Blessed One and sat down respectfully apart.

And the Blessed One said to Visakha Migaramata, as she sat thus apart; "Pray, how is it, Visakha, that you visit me thus at an unseasonable hour?" Just now, Sire, I was desirous of obtaining a favor from the King Pasenadi Kosala . . . [repetition. *Transl.*] but he did not accede to my request."

And the Blessed One in this connection, on that occasion, breathed forth this solemn utterance:--

*"All weakness is pain, all power is happiness:*
*When some struggle has to be encountered, men grieve:*
*It is hard to escape from the bondage thereof."*

10. Thus have I heard. On a certain occasion the Blessed One dwelt at Anupiya, in the mango grove.

At that time, the venerable Bhaddiya, the son of Kaligodha was in the habit of roaming through the forests, sitting at the foot of trees and frequenting desolate places. And he repeatedly exclaimed these emotional words; "Ah, Happiness, Ah, Happiness."

And a number of Bhikkhus heard the venerable Bhaddiya repeatedly exclaiming the emotional words, "Ah, Happiness, Ah, Happiness", as he wandered through the forests, under trees and in desolate places.

And when they heard him, they said to themselves; "Doubtless our friend the venerable Bhaddiya, who formerly enjoyed the comforts of a royal home, is unhappy since he adopted the religious life, and remembering the past, he now roams through the forests, under trees and in desolate places, repeatedly exclaiming the emotional words: "Ah, Happiness, Ah, Happiness." And a number of Bhikkhus went to where the Blessed One was and drawing near they saluted the Blessed One and sat down respectfully apart and while thus sitting, they told the Blessed One what they had seen and heard [Text repeats above description. *Transl.*].

And the Blessed One called one of the Bhikkhus to him and said; "Go, O Bhikkhu, and in my name summon the Bhikkhu Bhaddiya thus; 'The Master, friend Bhaddiya, has sent for you'."

"So be it, Sire", said that Bhikkhu in assent to the Blessed One and he went to where the venerable Bhaddiya, son of Kaligodha was, and drawing near, he said to him; "The Master, friend Bhaddiya, has sent for you."

"So be it, friend", said the venerable Bhaddiya in assent to that Bhikkhu and he went to where the Blessed One was, and drawing near, he saluted the Blessed One and sat down respectfully apart and the Blessed One said to the venerable Bhaddiya, as he sat there respectfully apart; "Is it true, what I hear, O Bhaddiya, that you wander through the forests [repetition as above] exclaiming these emotional words; 'Ah, Happiness, Ah, Happiness'?"

"Even so, Sire".

"What significance is there in this, as perceived by you, O Bhaddiya, that causes you to wander through forests? [repetition as above. *Transl.*].

"Formerly, Sire, when I was in the enjoyment of a royal home, I was guarded and closely protected both within and without the palace, within and without the city I was guarded and closely protected, within my country and beyond my country I was guarded and closely protected.

Thus guarded and closely watched, Sire, I lived in a state of anxiety, distrust and alarm; now, Sire, that I wander through the forests, under trees and in desolate places, I pass my days, fearless, at rest, confident, unalarmed, in comfort, unterrified, supported by gifts of food and garments from others, and with a heart free as that of a gazelle.

Clearly perceiving the significance of the matter, I chose, Sire, to wander through the forests, under trees and in desolate places, exclaiming those emotional words; 'Ah, Happiness, Ah, Happiness'."

And the Blessed One, in this connection, on that occasion, breathed forth this solemn utterance:--

*"With whom there is no annoy, who has overcome birth and rebirth in this world,*
*Such a one, free from fear, happy and griefless,*
*Comes not within the ken of the gods."*

# CHAPTER III. "NANDA".

1. Thus have I heard. On a certain occasion the Blessed One dwelt at Savatthi, in the Jetavana, the garden of Anâthapindika.

Now at that time a certain Bhikkhu, was sitting, not far from the Blessed One, in a cross-legged position, with body erect; and mindful and conscious, he bore without a murmur, acute, piercing and terrible pains, the result of deeds done in the past.

And the Blessed One beheld that Bhikkhu, sitting not far off, in a cross-legged position, with body erect, mindful and conscious, and bearing without a murmur, acute, piercing and terrible pains, the result of deeds done in the past.

And the Blessed One, in this connection, on that occasion, breathed forth this solemn utterance:--

*"The Bhikkhu who is freed from Karma,*
*Who has shaken off the dust (of sin) accumulated in the past,*
*Who has suppressed the notion 'this is mine',*
*For such a one, there is no cause to lament."*

2. Thus have I heard. On a certain occasion the Blessed One dwelt at Savatthi, in the Jetavana, the garden of Anâthapindika.

Now at that time the venerable Nanda, a cousin of the Blessed One, said to a number of Bhikkhus; "Friends, I am unhappy, leading the religious life, I am unable to bear (the burden of) a religious life, I intend to abandon the precepts and return to the lower life."

And a certain Bhikkhu went to where the Blessed One was and drawing near he saluted the Blessed One and sat down respectfully apart and while thus sitting he said to the Blessed One: "Sire, the venerable Nanda, a cousin of the Blessed One, has spoken to a number of Bhikkhus, saying: "I am unhappy etc. [as above. *Transl.*]. I intend to return to the lower life."

And the Blessed One called one of the Bhikkhus to him and said: "Go, thou, and in my name summon the Bhikkhu Nanda here, saying, 'The Master, friend Nanda, has sent for you'."

"So be it, Sire", said that Bhikkhu in assent to the Blessed One and he went to where the venerable Nanda was, and drawing near said to the venerable Nanda: "The Master, brother Nanda, has sent for you." "So be it, brother," said the venerable Nanda in assent to that Bhikkhu and he went to where the Blessed One was and drawing near he saluted the Blessed One and sat down respectfully apart, and the Blessed One said to the venerable Nanda as he sat there apart: "Is it true, what I hear, O Nanda, that you have spoken to a number of Bhikkhus, saying: "I am unhappy etc. [as above. *Transl.*]. I intend to revert to the lower life?"

"Even so, Lord."

"How is it, Nanda, that you are unhappy, leading the religious life, and intend to abandon the precepts and revert to the lower life?"

"O, Sire, a daughter of the Sakya race, the fairest maid in all the land, looking out (of the window) with hair half-braided, called out to me, as I was leaving my house, 'Delay not, Sir, thy return'. So calling her to mind, Sire, I am unhappy leading the religious life, I am unable to support the burden of a religious life and intend to abandon the precepts and revert to the lower life."

Then the Blessed One taking the venerable Nanda by the arm, and just as if a strong man should outstretch his bent arm or draw back his outstretched arm, even thus he vanished from the Jetavana and reappeared in the heaven of the "Great Thirty-Three".

Now at that time some 500 pink-footed celestial nymphs had arrived to minister to Sakka the king of the gods.

Then the Blessed One called the venerable Nanda to him and said: "Do you not see, Nanda, these 500 pink-footed celestial nymphs?"

"Even so, Sire."

"What do you think, Nanda, which is the most beautiful, the most lovely, the most entrancing, that daughter of the Sakya race, the fairest maid in all the land or these 500 pink-footed celestial nymphs?"

"It is, Sire, as if she was a singed she-monkey, with ears and nose cut off. The daughter of the Sakya race, the fairest maid in all the land, is not to be reckoned with these 500 pink-footed celestial nymphs, she is not worth a fraction of them, not worth having. These 500 pink-footed celestial nymphs are the most beautiful, the most lovely, the most entrancing." "Rejoice then, Nanda, rejoice, for I will guarantee you the possession of those 500 pink-footed celestial nymphs."

"If the Blessed One will guarantee me the possession of these 500 pink-footed nymphs, I shall lead, Sire, the religious life in happiness."

Then the Blessed One taking the venerable Nanda by the arm, just as if a strong man should outstretch his bent arm and bend back his outstretched arm, even thus he vanished from the heaven of the "Great Thirty-Three" and reappeared in the Jetavana.

And the Bhikkhus heard a report that the venerable Nanda, the cousin of the Blessed One, was leading the religious life because he had been promised celestial nymphs, for it was said that the Blessed One had guaranteed him the possession of 500 pink-footed celestial nymphs.

And the Bhikkhus, the companions of the venerable Nanda, called the venerable Nanda, a slave, a mean person; saying: "This venerable Nanda is a slave, a mean person. This venerable Nanda, we hear, leads the religious life for the sake of celestial nymphs. The Blessed One, we hear, has guaranteed him the possession of 500 pink-footed celestial nymphs."

And the venerable Nanda saddened, humiliated, and rendered despicable by the abuse of his companions, who called him a drudge and a mean person,--alone, remote from the haunts of men, ardent, resolute, self possessed, not long afterwards, for the sake of which scions of noble families abandon their homes for the homeless state, he, acquiring by himself and realizing the higher knowledge, attained, in this very existence, to the supreme consummation of a holy life. He knew that rebirth was at an end, the religious life had been lived, that which ought to he done had been done: "I have finished with this world."

And the venerable Nanda hecame yet another of the Arahats.

When the night was far spent, certain celestial beings of dazzling beauty, illuminating the whole of the Jetavana with their radiance, went to where the Blessed One was and drawing near, they saluted the Blessed One and stationed themselves respectfully apart and while thus standing, those celestial beings said to the Blessed One; "The venerable Nanda, Sire, the cousin of the Blessed One, by the destruction of the sins, has acquired by himself and realized the higher Knowledge, and in this very existence, he experiences the joy of a heart set free, and of that emancipation which springs from wisdom."

And to the Blessed One also had come the knowledge that the venerable Nanda, by the destruction of the sins etc. [as above. *Transl.*]. And at the end of that night the venerable Nanda went to where the Blessed One was, and drawing near he saluted the Blessed One and sat down respectfully apart, and while thus sitting the venerable Nanda said to the Blessed One; "Sire, the Blessed One guaranteed to give me the possession of 500 pink-footed celestial nymphs; I now release the Blessed One from that promise." "With my own mind, Nanda, I have grasped what is in your heart and know that Nanda by the destruction of the sins etc. [as above. *Transl.*]." The gods also have told me thus; "The venerable Nanda, by the destruction of the sins etc. [as above. *Transl.*]. "Since, Nanda, your heart is freed from 'attachment' and the sins, I too am released from that promise."

And the Blessed One in this connection, on that occasion, breathed forth this solemn utterance:--

*"He who has crossed the slough of impurity,*
*Who has crushed the thorns of desire,*
*That Bhikkhu, whether there be ease or discomfort,*
*Is at peace."*

3. Thus have I heard. On a certain occasion the Blessed One dwelt at Savatthi, in the Jetavana, the garden of Anâthapindika.

Now at that time some 500 Bhikkhus, with Yasoja at their head, came to see the Blessed One.

And these newly arrived Bhikkhus, while interchanging courtesies with the resident Bhikkhus and arranging their sleeping places, alms-bowls and garments, created a great uproar.

And the Blessed One called the venerable Ananda to him and said; "Who, Ananda, are these noisy and uproarious people? One would suppose they were fishermen catching fish."

"Sire, some 500 Bhikkhus, with Yasoja at their head, have come to Savatthi to see the Blessed One. And these newly arrived Bhikkhus while exchanging courtesies with the resident Bhikkhus and arranging their sleeping places, alms-bowls and garments, are creating this uproar."

"Then in my name, Ananda, call those Bhikkhus here, saying, 'Reverend Sirs, the Master has sent for you'."

"So be it, Sire;" said Ananda in assent to the Blessed One and he went to where those Bhikkhus were, and drawing near, he said to those Bhikkhus; "Reverend Sirs, the Master has sent for you."

"So be it, brother;" said those Bhikkhus in assent to the venerable Ananda and they went to where the Blessed One was, and drawing near, they saluted the Blessed One and sat down respectfully apart, and the Blessed One said to them as they sat there; "What is the meaning of this noise and uproar? One would suppose you were fishermen catching fish."

When these words had been spoken, the venerable Yasoja said to the Blessed One; "These newly arrived Bhikkhus etc. [as above. *Transl.*] are creating this uproar."

"I direct you to leave, O Bhikkhus; it is not fitting that you should converse with me."

"So be it, Sire;" said those Bhikkhus in assent to the Blessed One and they arose from their seats and saluted the Blessed One, and passing round keeping their right sides to him, they packed up their bedding and taking with them their alms-bowls and tunics, they departed for the country of the Vajjis, and as they journeyed on through the country of the Vajjis they came to the river Vaggumuda and when they arrived there, they built for themselves leaf-huts on the banks of the river Vaggumuda and spent the rainy season there.

And the venerable Yasoja, who spent the rainy season there, called the Bhikkhus to him and said; "Friends, the Blessed One has directed us hither, desirous of our good and welfare, out of mercy and in compassion for us. Now, friends, we should so live, that the Blessed One may be pleased with our manner of living."

"Even so, brother"; said those Bhikkhus in assent. And these Bhikkhus, living remote from the haunts of men, unflagging in zeal, ardent, restrained, within the duration of the rainy season, attained to the 'threefold knowledge'.

And the Blessed One having tarried at Savatthi as long as it was agreeable to him, set forth on his way to Vesali, and wandering from place to place he arrived at Vesali.

And the Blessed One lodged at Vesali in the Pagoda Hall, in the Mahavana.

And the Blessed One, having grasped with his own mind what was in the thoughts of those Bhikkhus, called the venerable Ananda to him and said; "It seems to me, Ananda, as if this quarter of the earth had become illuminated, had become radiant with light, it occurs to me as an agreeable idea to go to where those Bhikkhus live on the banks of the Vaggumuda. Send, Ananda, a messenger to those Bhikkhus on the banks of the Vaggumuda; 'the Master sends for the reverend brethren, the Master desires to see the reverend brethren'."

"So be it, Sire;" said the venerable Ananda in assent to the Blessed One and he went to where a certain Bhikkhu was and drawing near, he said to that Bhikkhu; "Go, thou, friend, to where the Bhikkhus live on the banks of the Vaggumuda and say to them; 'the master sends for the reverend brethren, the master desires to see the reverend brethren'."

"So be it, brother;" said that Bhikkhu in assent to the venerable Ananda, and just as if a strong man should stretch out his bent arm or bend back his outstretched arm, even thus he vanished from the Pagoda Hall in the Mahavana, and reappeared in the presence of those Bhikkhus on the banks of the river Vaggumuda.

And that Bhikkhu said to the Bhikkhus on the banks of the river Vaggumuda: "The Master sends for the reverend brethren, the Master desires to see the reverend brethren."

"So be it, brother;" said those Bhikkhus in assent to that Bhikkhu and packing up their bedding and taking with them their alms-bowls and tunics--just as if a strong man etc. [as above. *Transl.*]--even thus, they vanished from the banks of the river Vaggumuda and reappeared at the Pagoda Hall in the Mahavana, face to face with the Blessed One.

Now at that time the Blessed One was sitting in a state of motionless trance.

And those Bhikkhus said to themselves: "The Blessed One is in a motionless state;" and they all sat down in a motionless state of trance. And the venerable Ananda, as the first watch of the advancing night was passing arose from his seat, and placing his tunic upon one shoulder only (leaving the other bare) went to where the Blessed One was and stretching forth his hands said to the Blessed One: "Sire, the night is advanced, the first watch is passing, the newly arrived Bhikkhus have waited long. May it please the Blessed One to exchange courtesies with the newly arrived Bhikkhus."

When these words had been spoken, the Blessed One remained silent.

A second time the venerable Ananda, as the middle watch of the advancing night was passing, arose from his seat and placing his tunic upon one shoulder only went to where the Blessed One was, and stretching forth his hands said to the Blessed One: "Sire, the night is advancing, the middle watch is passing; the newly arrived Bhikkhus have waited long. May it please the Blessed One to exchange courtesies with the newly arrived Bhikkhus."

A second time, the Blessed One remained silent. A third time the venerable Ananda, as the last watch of the advancing night was passing, and the dawn arising, and the night far spent, got up from his seat and placing his tunic upon one shoulder only, went to where the Blessed One was, and stretching forth his hands, said to the Blessed One: "Sire, the night is advancing, the last watch is passing, dawn is arising, the night is far spent, the newly arrived Bhikkhus have waited long. May it please the Blessed One to exchange courtesies with the newly arrived Bhikkhus."

And the Blessed One arising from that state of trance, called the venerable Ananda to him and said: "If, Ananda, you know, you should not reply to them: I and all these 500 Bhikkhus have sat in a state of motionless trance."

And the Blessed One, in this connection, on that occasion, breathed forth this solemn utterance:--

*"He who has overcome the thorns of desire,*
*Who has overcome abuse and stripes and imprisonment,*
*He stands firm as a mountain,*
*Whether there be ease or discomfort,*
*That Bhikkhu trembles not."*

4. Thus have I heard. On a certain occasion the Blessed One dwelt at Savatthi in the Jetavana, the garden of Anâthapindika.

Now at that time, the venerable Sariputta sat, not far from the Blessed One, in a cross-legged position, with body erect, placing memory directly before him. And the Blessed One saw the venerable Sariputta as he sat, not far off, in a cross-legged position, with body erect, placing memory directly before him. And the Blessed One, in this connection, on that occasion, breathed forth this solemn utterance:--

*"As the mountain rock unshaken stands*
*So, delusion slain, the Bhikkhu*
*Like to a mountain, trembles not."*

5. Thus have I heard. On a certain occasion the Blessed One dwelt at Savatthi, in the Jetavana, the garden of Anâthapindika.

Now at that time the venerable Mahamoggallana was sitting, not far from the Blessed One, in a cross-legged position, with body erect, subjectively engaged in meditation on the body.

And the Blessed One saw the venerable Mahamoggalana etc. [as above. *Transl.*] subjectively engaged in meditation on the body.

And the Blessed One, in this connection, on that occasion, breathed forth this solemn utterance:

*"He who is engaged in meditation on the body,*
*Who is restrained as to the 'five realms' of contact,*
*That Bhikkhu, ever tranquil, will realize his own deliverance."*

6. Thus have I heard. On a certain occasion the Blessed One dwelt at Râjagaha, in the Bambu Grove, in Kalandikanivapa.

Now at that time the venerable Pilindavaccha was in the habit of reviling the Bhikkhus and calling them outcasts (Vasalas).

And a number of Bhikkhus went to where the Blessed One was, and drawing near, they saluted the Blessed One and sat down respectfully apart, and while thus sitting they said to the Blessed One; "Sire, the venerable Pilindavaccha is in the habit of reviling the Bhikkhus and calling them outcasts (Vasalas)."

And the Blessed One called one of the Bhikkhus to him and said: "Go, thou Bhikkhu, and in my name summon hither the Bhikkhu Pilindavaccha and say "Brother, the Master sends for you."

"So be it, Sire;" said that Bhikkhu in assent to the Blessed One and he went to where the venerable Pilindavaccha was, and drawing near, he said to Pilindavaccha; "The Master, brother, sends for you."

"So be it, brother;" said the venerable Pilindavaccha in assent to that Bhikkhu and he went to where the Blessed One was and drawing near, he saluted the Blessed One and sat down respectfully apart, and the Blessed One said to him as he sat there; "Is it true, Vaccha, what I hear, that you are in the habit of calling the Bhikkhus outcasts (Vasalas)?"

"Even so, Lord."

And the Blessed One calling to mind the former existence of Pilindavaccha said to the Bikkhus; "Molest not, O Bhikkhus, the Bhikkhu Vaccha. There is no guilt to be found in Vaccha, O Bhikkhus, in that he addresses the Bhikkhus as outcasts. In five hundred previous existences the Bhikkhu Vaccha was born, as one of low caste, in a Brahmin family. He contracted this habit of abuse long ago. Hence it is the custom of this Vaccha to call the Bhikkhus outcasts."

And the Blessed One, in this connection, on that occasion, breathed forth this solemn utterance:--

*"From whom no deceit or pride proceeds,*
*In whom avarice is annihilated,*
*Who has got rid of the notion 'this is mine',*
*Who is passionless and has put away wrath,*
*Who is freed from all cares,*
*That Bhikkhu is a Brahmana and a Samana."*

7. Thus have I heard. On a certain occasion the Blessed One dwelt at Râjagaha, in the Bambu Grove, in Kalandikanivâpa.

Now at that time the venerable Mahakassapa who lived in the Pipphali cave, had been sitting for seven days in a cross-legged position, and entered into a state of trance.

And the venerable Mahakassapa, at the end of the seventh day, arose from that state of trance.

And when he arose from that state of trance, this thought occurred to the venerable Mahakassapa; "what if I were to go to Râjagaha in search of alms."

Now at that time there were some 500 Devas zealously employed in obtaining alms for the venerable Mahakassapa. And the venerable Mahakassapa, dismissing those 500 Devas, put on his robe, in the forenoon, and taking his alms-bowl and tunic, entered Râjagaha for alms.

At that time Sakka, the King of the Devas, anxious to present alms to the venerable Mahakassapa took upon himself the form of a weaver and wove. Sujâtâ Asurakanna filled, etc..

And the venerable Mahakassapa, wandering from house to house in search of alms, drew near to the dwelling place of Sakka, King of the Devas, and Sakka, King of the Devas, seeing from afar the approach of the venerable Mahakassapa, left his house and received him with honor; and relieving him of his alms bowl, took him into his house. And he took boiled rice out of a jar with his hand and filled the alms bowl and presented it to the venerable Mahakassapa. With the rice there was a great variety of soups and sauces and many juicy concoctions.

And this thought occurred to the venerable Mahakassapa: "Who can this person be, who possesses such magical powers?"

And this thought also occurred to the venerable Mahakassapa: "Can it be that this is Sakka, King of the Devas?"

And perceiving it to be Sakka, King of the Devas, he said to him, "you have done this, O Kosiya; do not such a thing again."

"Revered Kassapa, for us even there is need of meritorious actions, by us even meritorious deeds should be performed."

And Sakka, King of the Devas, saluted the venerable Kassapa and passing round keeping his right side to him, rose into the air and three times from his place in the sky uttered these ecstatic words: "O, charity, supreme charity, set up by Kassapa."

And the Blessed One, with his divine, clear sense of hearing, surpassing that of men, heard Sakka, King of the Devas, uttering, three times, from his place in the sky, the ecstatic words: "O Charity, Supreme Charity, set up by Kassapa."

And the Blessed One, in this connection, on that occasion, breathed forth this solemn utterance:--

*"The Bhikkhu who receives alms in conformity to the rules,*
*Who nurtures and cherishes the lonely ones,*
*Such a one, ever mindful and serene, the gods envy."*

8. Thus have I heard. On a certain occasion the Blessed One dwelt at Savatthi, in the Jetavana, the garden of Anâthapindika.

Now at that time a large number of Bhikkhus having returned from their rounds and finished their meal, assembled and fell to their places in the Kareri Circular Hall, and a discussion arose to this effect: "The Bhikkhu, brothers, who conforms to the rules concerning alms, on going his rounds, is privileged to see, from time to time, with his eyes agreeable forms, to hear from time to time, with his ears agreeable sounds, to perceive from time to time with his nose agreeable perfumes, to taste from time to time with his tongue agreeable tastes, and to come in contact from time to time with bodies pleasant to touch. The Bhikkhu, brothers, who conforms to the rules concerning alms, while going on his rounds, is honoured, respected, held in reverence, esteemed and looked up to. Come now, brothers, let us also conform to the rules concerning alms, and then we too will be privileged to see from time to time with our eyes agreeable forms, to hear from time to time with our ears agreeable sounds, to perceive from time to time with our noses agreeable perfumes, to taste from time to time with our tongues agreeable tastes, and to come in contact from time to time with bodies pleasant to touch. We, too, while going our rounds will be honoured, respected, held in reverence, esteemed and looked up to." Such was the subject of discussion and dispute that engaged those Bhikkhus.

And the Blessed One, arising from his solitary communings at eventide, went to where the Kareri Circular Hall was and when he arrived there, he sat down on the appointed seat and while thus sitting, he called the Bhikkhus to him and said: "What, O Bhikkhus, is the nature of the discussion, what is the dispute, that has arisen amongst you assembled here?"

Just now, Sire, we assembled and fell into our places in the Kareri Circular Hall after going our rounds and a discussion took place to the following effect; [as above. *Transl.*]. "This was the subject of discussion and dispute when the Blessed One arrived."

"It is not fitting, O Bhikkhus, for such as you, scions of noble families, who through faith have abandoned your homes for the homeless state, to be occupied in such discussions. When you assemble and fall into your places, one of two courses should be pursued, either righteous converse, or a noble silence."

And the Blessed One, in this connection, on that occasion, breathed forth this solemn utterance:--

*"The Bhikkhu who conforms to the rules concerning alms,*

*Who is a nurturer and cherisher of the lonely,*
*Him the gods envy, not if his heart is set on fame and honour."*

9. Thus have I heard. On a certain occasion the Blessed One dwelt at Savatthi, in the Jetavana, the garden of Anâthapindika.

Now at that time a number of Bhikkhus [as above. *Transl.*] and a dispute arose thus; "Who, brothers, is proficient in the arts, who trains himself in the arts, which is the greatest of the arts?"

Some said; "Skill in the management of elephants;" some said, "Skill in the management of horses, of vehicles;" others said, "Skill in the manufacture of bows, of sword hilts; skill in conveyancing, in mathematics, in estimates, in engraving, in poetry, in casuistry, in agriculture."

Such was the subject of dispute that arose amongst these Bhikkhus.

And the Blessed One, arising at eventide from his solitary communings [as above. *Transl.*], said; "what is the nature of the dispute that has arisen amongst you?" [as above. *Transl.*].

This was the subject of discussion and dispute when the Blessed One arrived.

"It is not fitting, O Bhikkhus, [as above] etc. One of two causes should be pursued, either righteous converse or a noble silence."

And the Blessed One, in this connection, on that occasion, breathed forth this solemn utterance:--

*"Verily he who is skilled not in the arts, who is desirous of good, with senses stilled, wholly free,*
*Who goes homeless, in whom the notion 'this is mine' is not,*
*Who is passion free,*
*That Bhikkhu having slain the Tempter, walks alone (independent of skill in the arts)."*

10. Thus have I heard. On a certain occasion the Exalted One, soon after the attainment of Buddhahood, dwelt at Uruvela, on the banks of the stream Neranjara, at the foot of the tree of Enlightenment.

Now at that time the Exalted One had sat for seven days in an attitude of meditation and was experiencing the bliss of Emancipation.

And the Exalted One, at the end of the seventh day, arose from the state of trance and surveyed the world with the eyes of a Buddha.

And the Exalted One surveying the world with the eyes of a Buddha, saw beings burnt by many fires, consumed by grief, sins and delusions.

And the Exalted One, in this connection, on that occasion breathed forth this solemn utterance:--

*"This world is a consuming fire. The people are sunk in 'Contact,' they proclaim disease as something good.*
*What a man supposes will happen, the opposite to that happens.*
*This people, who differentiate themselves, having attained to existence, sunk in existence, praise existence.*

*When a man praises it, there is fear: where there is fear, there is sorrow.*

*The complete abandonment (of the love) of existence: that is called the holy life.*

*All these Samanas and Brahmanas who say that by existence there is escape from existence, these, I declare, will not escape from existence.*

*But all these Samanas and Brahmanas who say that by non-existence there is escape from existence, these, I declare, are independent of existence.*

*Not from Upadhi, as a result, does sorrow arise: when all 'attachment' is destroyed, then is there no resurgence of sorrow.*

*Behold this variegated world, sunk in ignorance, full of pleasure-loving beings, unemancipated!*

*All existence, whatever or wherever, is impermanent, full of sorrow and subject to change."*

# CHAPTER IV. "MEGHIYA."

1. Thus have I heard. On a certain occasion the Blessed One dwelt at Calaka, on the Calaka mountain.

Now at that time the venerable Meghiya was the servitor of the Blessed One. And the venerable Meghiya went to where the Blessed One was and drawing near, he saluted the Blessed One and stationed himself respectfully apart, and while thus standing the venerable Meghiya said to the Blessed One: "I wish, Sire, to enter the village of Jantu to go on my rounds for alms."

"Very well, Meghiya, do as you think fit."

And the venerable Meghiya clothing himself in the forenoon and taking his alms-bowl and tunic entered the Jantu village for alms. And when he had gone his rounds and finished his meal, he went to the banks of the Kimikâla-river and as he wandered on foot from place to place along the banks of the river, he beheld an enchanting and delightful Grove of Mango-trees. And when he saw it, he exclaimed: "How beautiful, how lovely is this Mango Grove! Truly this is a fitting place for a scion of noble family to struggle and strive (after holiness). If the Blessed One consents, I will return to this Mango Grove and there struggle and strive (after holiness)."

And the venerable Meghiya went to where the Blessed One was and drawing near, he saluted the Blessed One and sat down respectfully apart and while thus sitting, he said to the Blessed One: "In the forenoon, Sire, having put on my garments and taking my alms-bowl and tunic, I entered the Jantu village for alms, and when I had gone my rounds and finished my meal, I went to the banks of the Kimikâla-river and wandering on foot from place to place I beheld an enchanting and delightful Grove of Mango-trees and when I saw it, I exclaimed: 'How lovely, how beautiful is this Mango Grove! Surely this is a fitting place for a scion of noble family, to struggle and strive (after holiness)'. If the Blessed One will consent, I will return to this Mango Grove and struggle and strive (after holiness)."

"If, Sire, the Blessed One consents I will go to that Mango Grove and enter into the struggle."

When these words had been spoken, the Blessed One said to the venerable Meghiya: "Wait, for the present, Meghiya, we are alone now, at least till some other Bhikkhu arrives."

And a second time the venerable Meghiya spoke to the Blessed One, saying: "No further duties, Sire, have to be performed by the Blessed One, no further experience is needed, but I, Sire, have duties still to perform, and experience to gain. If, Sire, the Blessed One consents, I will go to that Mango Grove and enter upon the struggle."

A second time, the Blessed One said to the venerable Meghiya: "Wait a while, Meghiya, we are alone now, at least till some other Bhikkhu arrives."

A third time the venerable Meghiya said to the Blessed One: [As above. *Transl.*].

"As to the struggle, Meghiya, in what terms shall I declare it to you? Do now, Meghiya, as you think best."

And the venerable Meghiya arose from his seat and saluted the Blessed One and passing round keeping his right side to him, he went to where the Mango Grove was, and drawing near he entered the Mango Grove and sat down during the heat of the day at the foot of a tree.

And while living in that Mango Grove, the venerable Meghiya was constantly assailed by three kinds of evil and unlawful thoughts, namely lustful thoughts, malicious thoughts, and cruel thoughts.

And the venerable Meghiya thought to himself: "How strange is it, how marvellous is it, that I, who through faith have abandoned my home for the homeless state, should be filled with these these evil and unlawful thoughts, namely, lustful thoughts, malicious thoughts, and cruel thoughts."

And the venerable Meghiya arose from his solitary communings and went to where the Blessed One was and having saluted the Blessed One, he sat down respectfully apart and while thus sitting he said to the Blessed One: "while living in that Mango Grove, Sire, I was assailed by three evil and unlawful thoughts, namely lustful thoughts, malicious thoughts and cruel thoughts and I thought how strange, how marvellous is it, that I who through faith have abandoned my home for the homeless state, should be assailed by these three evil and unlawful thoughts.

"For the immaturely released heart, O Meghiya, five conditions conduce to maturity. What are these five?

1°. In this world, Meghiya, a Bhikkhu should have a virtuous friend, a virtuous companion. For the immaturely released heart, Meghiya, this is the first condition which conduces to maturity.

2°. Further, Meghiya, a Bhikkhu shonld be pious, should live a life of restraint according to the precepts, and be endued with right conduct, perceiving danger in the least of the sins, and adopting the moral precepts, should exercise himself therein, For the immaturely released heart, Meghiya, this is the second condition which conduces to maturity.

3°. Further, Meghiya, there should be discourses such as tend to the eradication of evil, to a beneficial expansion of the heart, to an utter weariness of the world, to the cessation of all desire, to tranquillity, to the higher knowledge, to supreme enlightenment, to Nirvana, that is, discourses on frugality, on contentment, solitude, exclusiveness, effort and exertion, piety, self-concentration, wisdom and emancipation as resulting from insight acquired by knowledge--by means of such discourses satisfaction is obtained, and trouble and difficulties overcome.

For the immaturely released heart, Meghiya, this is the third condition which conduces to maturity.

4°. Further, Meghiya, the Bhikkhu should live a life of effort and exertion, abandoning unlawful practises, he should practise what is lawful, he should be resolute, put forth his strength, not throwing down the burden in the practise of those things that are lawful.

For the immaturely released heart, Meghiya, this is the fourth condition which conduces to maturity.

5°. Further, Meghiya, the Bhikkhu should have wisdom, should be endowed with a knowledge of the 'rise and set' of things, of sublime penetration, and of that which leads to the complete cessation of sorrow.

For the immaturely released heart, Meghiya, this is the fifth condition which conduces to maturity.

For the immaturely released heart, Meghiya, these are the five conditions which conduce to maturity.

Thus, Meghiya, when the Bhikkhu has provided himself with a virtuous friend, a virtuous companion, a virtuous associate, it is to be expected that he will become pious, that he will live a life of restraint according to the precepts and be endued with right conduct, and seeing danger in the least of the sins, will adopt the moral precepts and exercise himself therein; and those discourses which tend to the eradication of evil, to a beneficial expansion of the heart, to an utter weariness of the world, to the cessation of all desire, to tranquillity, to the higher knowledge, to supreme enlightenment, to Nirvana, namely, discourses on frugality, contentment, solitude, exclusiveness, effort and exertion, piety, self-concentration, wisdom and emancipation resulting from insight acquired by knowledge--by the means of such discourses satisfaction is obtained and trouble and difficulties overcome.

Thus the Bhikkhu with a virtuous friend, a virtuous companion, a virtuous associate will live a life of effort and exertion, and abandoning unlawful practises will practise what is lawful, he will be resolute, put forth his strength and not throw down the burden in the practise of what is lawful.

Thus the Bhikkhu with a virtuous friend, a virtuous companion, a virtuous associate, will become wise, will be endowed with a knowledge of the 'rise and set' of things, of sublime penetration, and of that which conduces to the complete cessation of sorrow.

Moreover, Meghiya, the Bhikkhu who holds to these five conditions, must give special attention to four other conditions; in order to abandon lust he must dwell on the impurity (of the body), in order to forsake malice he must dwell on kindness, with a view to the excision of (evil) thoughts, he must practise meditation by (counting) inhalations and exhalations; for the removal of the pride which says 'I am', he must exercise himself in the consciousness of the impermanency of all things. By the consciousness of impermanence, the consciousness of non-egoity is established, and he who

31

is conscious of non-egoity succeeds in the removal of the notion 'I am', and in this very existence attains to Nirvana."

And the Blessed One, in this connection, on that occasion, breathed forth this solemn utterance:--

*"He who judges not aright these mean and subtle thoughts,*
*Whereby the mind is puffed up and inflated,*
*Such a one wanders in confusion from birth to birth.*
*But the wise man, ardent and mindful who keeps such thoughts in subjection.*
*He escapes from the thoughts which puff up and inflate the mind."*

2. Thus have I heard. On a certain occasion the Blessed One dwelt at Kusinara, in the Upavattana, the Sâl forest of the Mallas.

Now at that time there lived, not far from the Blessed One, a great number of Bhikkhus in huts set up in the forest.

They were puffed up, proud, fickle, garrulous, loose in their talk, thoughtless, without knowledge, unrestrained, scatter-brained and sensuous.

And the Blessed One beheld these Bhikkhus living in huts set up in the forest, puffed up, fickle, garrulous, loose in their talk, thoughtless, without knowledge, unrestrained, scatter-brained and sensuous.

And the Blessed One, in this connection, on that occasion, breathed forth this solemn utterance:--

*"He who keeps not watch over his body,*
*Who is under the spell of false doctrines,*
*Who succumbs to sloth and torpor,*
*Such a one passes into the power of the Tempter.*
*But he who keeps watch over his mind,*
*Whose sphere is right thoughts,*
*Who sets ever before him right doctrine,*
*Who knows the 'rise and set' of things,*
*Who overcomes sloth and torpor,*
*That Bhikkhu escapes from all states of punishment."*

3. Thus have I heard. On a certain occasion, the Blessed One with a large gathering of the Brotherhood, was wandering about from place to place in the Kosala-country. Now at that time the Blessed One having left the road, went to the foot of a tree and sat down on the appointed seat.

And a certain herdsman approached the Blessed One, and drawing near, saluted the Blessed One and sat down apart and as the herdsman sat there, the Blessed One, instructed, animated, incited and gladdened him with righteous discourse.

And the herdsman, instructed, animated, incited and gladdened by the righteous discourse of the Blessed One said: "May it please the Blessed One and the brethren to take their morrow's meal with me?"

And the Blessed One assented by his silence.

And the herdsman, perceiving that the Blessed One had assented, arose from his seat and saluted the Blessed One, and passing round keeping his right side to him, he departed. And the herdsman at the end of that night having caused to be prepared in his own house an abundance of gruel and butter-milk announced to the Blessed One that the time had come saying: "Sire, the time is come, the meal is ready."

And the Blessed One, robing himself in the forenoon and taking his alms-bowl and tunic, went, together with the Brotherhood, to where the herdsman's house was and when he arrived there, he sat down on the appointed seat.

And the herdsman with his own hands served and offered to the brethren, with the Buddha at their head, the gruel and the butter-milk. And when the Blessed One had finished his meal and withdrawn his hand from the bowl, the herdsman taking a low seat, sat down respectfully apart and while he was thus sitting, the Blessed One instructed, animated, incited and gladdened the herdsman with righteous discourse. And the Blessed One arose from his seat and departed. Not long after the departure of the Blessed One, a certain man, (in a feud) connected with a woman, took the life of the herdsman.

And a number of Bhikkhus went to where the Blessed One was and drawing near they saluted the Blessed One and sat down respectfully apart, and while thus sitting, they said to the Blessed One: "That herdsman it is said, Sire, who lately served and offered to the Fraternity with the Buddha at their head, gruel and butter-milk, has been killed by a man, in connection with some quarrel about a woman. And the Blessed One, in this connection, on that occasion, breathed forth this solemn utterance:--

*"Whatever an enemy may do to an enemy*
*Or an angry man to an angry man,*
*A mind intent on what is wrong,*
*Works evil worse."*

4. On a certain occasion the Blessed One dwelt at Râjagaha, in the Bambu Grove, in Kalandikanivapa.

Now at that time the venerable Sariputta and the venerable Moggalana the Great were living at the Kapotakandara monastery.

And the venerable Sariputta while sitting, with lately shaven hair, in the open air, on a moonlit night, fell into a trance.

And two Yakkhas, who were associates, came from the north country to the south country, to transact some business. And when these Yakkhas observed the venerable Sariputta, sitting in the open air, in the moonlit night, with lately shaven hair, the first Yakkha said to the second Yakkha: "It occurs to me, friend, to give this Samana a blow on the head." When these words had been spoken the second Yakkha said to his friend:

"Enough, friend, do not strike the Samana. A renowned man, is this Samana, very powerful and mighty in magic."

A second time the first Yakkha said to the second Yakkha: "It occurs to me, friend, to give this Samana a blow on the head."

A second time the second Yakkha replied: "Enough, friend, strike not the Samana. A renowned man is this Samana, very powerful and mighty in magic."

A third time the first Yakkha said to the second Yakkha: "It occurs to me, friend, to give this Samana a blow on the head."

And a third time the second Yakkha replied: "Enough, friend. A renowned man is this Samana, very powerful and mighty in magic."

And the first Yakkha, not heeding the second Yakkha, delivered a blow on the head of the venerable Sariputta; such a blow, moreover, as would fell an elephant 7 or 7½ cubits high or crush a huge mountain peak. And that Yakkha crying out, 'I burn, I burn', fell there and then, into the great Hell.

And the venerable Moggallana the Great beheld with his divinely clear vision, surpassing that of men, the blow delivered by the Yakkha on the head of the venerable Sariputta, and when he saw it, he went to where the venerable Sariputta was and drawing near, said to him: "I trust, brother, that you are at ease, that you are doing well, that there is no pain."

"I am at ease, brother Moggallana, and am doing well, but I feel a slight pain in my head."

"How strange is it, brother Sariputta! How marvellous is it, brother Sariputta! How great is the magical power, how great is the might of the venerable Sariputta!" Just now, brother Sariputta, a certain Yakkha delivered a blow on your head, and how great was that blow! With such a blow, indeed, one might fell an elephant 7 or 7½ cubits high and crush a huge mountain peak. And the venerable Sariputta says: 'I am at ease, friend Moggallana, I am doing well, friend Moggallana, I feel only a slight pain in my head'."

"It is strange, brother Moggallana, it is wonderful, brother Moggallana-- how great must be the magical power of the venerable Moggallana, that he saw a Yakkha at all. I did not see even a mud-sprite."

And the Blessed One with his divinely clear hearing, surpassing that of men, heard the conversation which took place between these two mighty heroes.

And the Blessed One, in this connection, on that occasion, breathed forth this solemn utterance:--

*"He whose heart, like a rock unshaken stands,*
*Who is passion free, not angry with the angry,*
*He whose heart is thus trained,*
*How shall pain come to such a one?"*

5. Thus have I heard. On a certain occasion the Blessed One dwelt at Kosambi in the Ghosita monastery.

Now at that time the Blessed One was living surrounded by a crowd of monks and nuns, of male and female lay disciples, of kings and their ministers, as well as by heretical sects and their pupils, and he suffered annoyance and discomfort.

And this thought occurred to him: "Surrounded by a crowd of monks and nuns, of male and female votaries, of kings and their ministers, as well as by heretical sects and their pupils, I suffer annoyance and discomfort. What if I were to live alone, remote from the crowd?"

And the Blessed One robing himself in the forenoon and taking his alms-bowl and tunic, entered Kosambi for alms. Having perambulated Kosambi for alms, he returned from his rounds and after finishing his meal, he himself put in order his sleeping place, and taking his alms-bowl and tunic, and without informing his servitor or giving notice to the Brethren, he departed, alone, without a companion, in the direction of Palileyyaka and wandering from place to place he reached Palileyyaka and took up his abode there.

And the Blessed One sojourned in the dense grove Rakkhilâ, in the vicinity of Palileyyaka, at the foot of the Bhadda Sâl tree.

Now a certain noble elephant lived there, who was much inconvenienced by a crowd of male and female elephants, young elephants and elephant calves. He had to feed on blades of grass with their tips broken off, and they ate the young branches which he himself had broken down. He had also to drink water that had been polluted and when he plunged (into the water) to cross over, the female elephants rubbed their bodies against him. In consequence of this crowd he was annoyed and lived ill at ease.

And this thought occurred to the noble elephant; "Surrounded by a crowd of male elephants and she elephants, young elephants and elephant calves, I have to feed on blades of grass with their tips broken off and they eat the young branches I myself have broken down. I have also to drink water that has been polluted and when I plunge (into the water) to cross over, the female elephants rub their bodies against me. In consequence of this crowd I am annoyed and live ill at ease. What if I were to live alone, remote from the crowd?"

And the noble elephant leaving the herd went to the deep groves of Rakkhita, in the vicinity of Palileyyaka, to the foot of the Bhadda Sâl tree, where the Blessed One was. And when he arrived there, he removed the grass from the spot which the Blessed One occupied, and brought with his trunk drinking water for the Blessed One.

And as the Blessed One was rejoicing in the calm of solitude and isolation, this thought arose; "Formerly, I lived a life of annoyance and discomfort surrounded by monks and nuns etc. [as above. *Transl.*]. Now no longer surrounded by monks and nuns etc. [as above. *Transl.*]. I live in comfort and at ease."

And in the mind of the noble elephant this thought arose: "Formerly, I lived a life of annoyance and discomfort surrounded by male elephants and she elephants etc. [as above. *Transl.*]. Now no longer surrounded I live in comfort and at ease."

And the Blessed One, with reference to his own solitude, and perceiving what was passing in the mind of that noble elephant, breathed forth this solemn utterance:--

*"The heart of the noble elephant (with tusks like plough-poles)*
*Is at one with the heart of the Noble One*
*For each delights in (the solitude of) the forest."*

6. Thus have I heard. On a certain occasion the Blessed One dwelt at Savatthi, in the Jetavana, the garden of Anâthapindika.

Now at that time the venerable Pindolabharadvâja was sitting, not far from the Blessed One in a cross-legged position, with body erect. He was a frequenter of forests, a recipient of alms, a weaver of clothes made of rags taken from a dust-heap, possessor of the three garments of a monk, content with little, satisfied, solitary, living apart from men, strenuous and eager, a keeper of the Dhutangas, and addicted to lofty thoughts.

And the Blessed One beheld the venerable Pindolabharadvâja, sitting not far off, in a cross-legged position, with body erect, a frequenter of forests, a recipient of alms, a wearer of clothes made of rags taken from a dust-heap, possessor of the three garments of a monk, content with little, satisfied, solitary, living apart from men, strenuous and eager, a keeper of the Dhutangas, and addicted to lofty thoughts.

And the Blessed One, in this connection, on that occasion, breathed forth this solemn utterance:--

*"To speak no ill, to injure not,*
*To be restrained according to the precepts,*
*To be temperate in food,*
*To sleep secluded,*
*To dwell on lofty thoughts,*
*This is the law of the Buddha."*

7. Thus have I heard. On a certain occasion the Blessed One dwelt at Savatthi, in the Jetavana, the garden of Anâthapindika.

Now at that time the venerable Sariputta was sitting, not far from the Blessed One, in a cross-legged position, with body erect, desiring little, content, a lover of solitude, living apart, strenuous and eager, and addicted to lofty thoughts.

And the Blessed One beheld the venerable Sariputta, sitting not far off, in a cross-legged position, with body erect, desiring little, content, a lover of solitude, living apart, strenuous and eager and addicted to lofty thoughts. And the Blessed One, in this connection, on that occasion, breathed forth this solemn utterance:--

*"The silent monk who dwells on lofty thoughts,*
*Who rejoices little,*
*Who is trained in the ways of silence;*
*To such a one, ever tranquil and mindful,*
*Sorrow comes not."*

8. Thus have I heard. On a certain occasion the Blessed One dwelt at Savatthi, in the Jetavana, the garden of Anâthapindika.

Now at that time the Blessed One was held in reverence, honoured, respected and esteemed, and was a recipient of the requisites of a monk of the Order, such as robes, alms, pallet, and medicines in case of sickness. The Brethren were also held in reverence, honoured, respected and esteemed and were recipients of the requisites of a monk, such as, robes, alms, pallet and medicines in case of sickness.

The wandering monks of the heretical sects were not held in reverence, etc. [as above. *Transl.*] and were not recipients of the requisites, [as above. *Transl.*]. And these wandering monks of the heretical sects could not endure the honour extended to the Blessed One and the Brethren, and they went to where the wandering nun Sundari was and drawing near they said to the wandering nun Sundari: "Is it in your power, Sister, to do something for your relatives?"

What am I to do, Sirs, what is it in my power to do? I am ready to sacrifice my life for my relatives."

"Then go at once, Sister, to the Jetavana."

"Be it so, Sirs," said Sundari the wandering nun in assent to these wandering monks of the heretical sects, and she went at once to the Jetavana.

And since these wandering monks of the heretical party knew that many people living in the Jetavana would have an opportunity of seeing the sudden arrival there of Sundari, the wandering nun, (they went there themselves) and (secretly) depriving her of life, threw her into a ruined well in the Jetavana. And they went to where the King Posenadi Kosala was, and drawing near they said to the King Posenadi Kosala; "great King, the wandering nun Sundari has disappeared."

"Where then do you suspect she is?"

"In the Jetavana, great King."

"Then search the Jetavana."

And those wandering monks of the heretical party searched in the Jetavana, and taking (the body) out of the ruined well into which it had been thrown, they placed it on a litter and brought it into Savatthi by the carriage road, and when they reached the place where the four roads meet, they caused a murmur amongst the people, by calling out: "Behold, Sirs, the work of the Sakya sons, shameless are these Sakya sons, impious, wicked, liars and depraved! They profess to be religious, pious, holy, truth speaking, virtuous and good men! There is nothing of the Samana in them, there is nothing of the Brahmana in them. There is no meaning in their Samana-ship, there is no meaning in their Brahmana-ship. Where is their Samana-ship, where is their Brahmana-ship? For how would a man who fulfils the duty of a man, deprive a woman of her life?" And the people of Savatthi, whenever they saw the Bhikkhus, reviled, abused, annoyed and worried them by using harsh and improper language, calling out: "Shameless are the Sakya sons, impious, wicked, liars and depraved!"

And a great number of Bhikkhus, having robed themselves in the forenoon, and taking their alms-bowls and tunics entered Savatthi for alms. And when they had gone their rounds in Savatthi and returned from receiving alms and finished their meal, they went to where the Blessed One was, and drawing near they saluted the Blessed One and sat down apart; and while thus sitting these Bhikkhus said to the Blessed One: "Whenever the people of Savatthi see the Bhikkhus, they revile, abuse, annoy and worry the Bhikkhus, by using harsh language and calling out; "Shameless are these Sakya sons, etc. [as above. *Transl.*].

"This uproar, O Bhikkhus, will not last long, it will last for seven days and at the end of the seventh day, it will subside. Therefore, O Bhikkhus, reprove those men of Savatthi, who, when they see you, revile, abuse etc. [as above. *Transl.*], with these verses:

*"The liar goes to hell, also he who having done an action, says 'I have not done it';*
*Hereafter there will be no distinction between them,*
*In another existence they will be men of base conduct."*

And these Bhikkhus having learnt by heart these verses in the presence of the Blessed One, reproved the men of Savatthi who reviled them with the above verses [abbreviation. *Transl.*].

And the people said to themselves: "These Samanas, these Sakya sons are unreasonable, we will have no more to do with these Sakya sons."

Thus the uproar did not last long, for seven days only did it last, and at the end of the seventh day it subsided.

And a number of Bhikkhus went to where the Blessed One was and drawing near, they saluted the Blessed One and sat down apart, and while thus sitting, they said to the Blessed One: "It is strange, Sire, it is marvellous, Sire! How well spoken were those words of the Blessed One: 'This uproar will not last long, for seven days will it last, at the end of the seventh day it will subside'. The uproar, Sire, has ceased."

And the Blessed One, in this connection, on that occasion, breathed forth this solemn utterance:--

*"The unrestrained pierce others with their words,*

*As one elephant pierces another elephant in battle.*
*When the Bhikkhu, of uncorrupted heart,*
*Hears the utterance of harsh words,*
*He bears them with resignation."*

9. Thus have I heard. On a certain occasion the Blessed One dwelt at Râjagaha, in the Bamboo Grove, in Kalandikanivâpa.

And there arose in the mind of the venerable Upasena, the son of Vanganta, this reflection, as he passed his days in solitude and seclusion: "How great is my gain, how great to me the advantage, that I have as Master, the Supreme Buddha, that I, under the discipline of the Doctrine so well taught, have abandoned my house for the homeless state, that I have, as holy companions, righteous and pious men, that I have fulfilled the precepts, that I am steadfast, tranquil in mind, an Arahat who has destroyed the sins, great in power, mighty in strength! Blessed to me is life, blessed is death!"

And the Blessed One grasping with his own mind the thoughts that were in the mind of the venerable Upasena, the son of Vanganta, in this connection, on that occasion, breathed forth this solemn utterance:--

*"He whom life torments not,*
*Who sorrows not at the approach of death,*
*If such a one is resolute and has seen Nirvana,*
*In the midst of grief, he is griefless.*
*The tranquil minded Bhikkhu, who has uprooted the thirst for existence,*
*By him the succession of births is ended,*
*He is reborn no more!"*

10. Thus have I heard. On a certain occasion the Blessed One dwelt at Savatthi, in the Jetavana, the garden of Anâthapindika.

Now at that time the venerable Sariputta was sitting, not far from the Blessed One, in a cross-legged position, with body erect, contemplating his own state of tranquillity.

And the Blessed One beheld the venerable Sariputta sitting, not far off, in a cross-legged position, with body erect, contemplating his own state of tranquillity.

And the Blessed One, in this connection, on that occasion, breathed forth this solemn utterance:--

*"The Bhikkhu whose mind is wholly calm,*
*Who has severed that which leads to a desire for existence,*
*By him the succession of births has been ended,*
*He is released from the bonds of the Wicked One."*

# CHAPTER V. SONA THERA.

1. On a certain occasion the Blessed One dwelt at Savatthi, in the Jetavana, the garden of Anâthapindika.

Now at that time the King Pasenadi Kosala, in company with the goddess Mallika, had ascended to his principal palace.

And the King Pasenadi Kosala said to the goddess Mallika:

"Do you, O Mallika, love any one better than yourself?"

"No, Great King, I love no one better than myself. Moreover, Great King, you do not love any one better than yourself."

"I too, O Mallika, love no one better than myself."

And the King Pasenadi Kosala, descending from his palace, went to where the Blessed One was, and drawing near, he saluted the Blessed One and sat down apart, and while thus seated, he said to the Blessed One: "Just now, Sire, I ascended to my principal palace, in company with the goddess Mallika and I said to the goddess Mallika: 'Do you love any one better than yourself Mallika?' etc. [as above. *Transl.*].

"I too, O Mallika, love no one better than myself."

And the Blessed One, in this connection, on that occasion, breathed forth this solemn utterance:--

*"As a man traversing the whole earth,*
*Finds not anywhere an object more loveable than himself;*
*Therefore, since the self is so universally loved by all,*
*The man who loves himself so much,*
*Should do no injury to others."*

2. Thus have I heard. On a certain occasion the Blessed One dwelt at Savatthi, in the Jetavana, the garden of Anâthapindika.

Now at that time the venerable Ananda, arising at eventide from his solitary communings, went to where the Blessed One was, and drawing near he saluted the Blessed One and sat down apart, and while thus sitting he said to the Blessed One: "How strange is it, Sire, how wonderful is it, Sire, that the mother of the Blessed One was so short-lived! On the seventh day from the birth of the Blessed One, the mother of the Blessed One died and was reborn in the retinue of the Tusita angels."

"So it is, Ananda, with the mothers of the Bodhisattas; they are short-lived and, on the seventh day after the birth of a Bodhisatta, they die, and are reborn in the retinue of the Tusita angels."

And the Blessed One, in this connection, on that occasion, breathed forth this solemn utterance:--

*"All beings that will be born,*
*All of them will depart leaving their bodies.*
*The wise man comprehending the decay of all things,*
*Should strive to lead a life of holiness."*

3. Thus have I heard. On a certain occasion the Blessed One was staying at Râjagaha, in the Bambu Grove, in Kalandikanivapa.

Now at that time there dwelt at Râjagaha, a leper, by name Suppabuddha, a mean, forlorn, miserable creature. It so happened that the Blessed One, surrounded by a large assembly of people, was at that time sitting there and teaching the Doctrine.

And the leper Suppabuddha beheld from afar off a number of people assembled, and when he beheld them, he thought to himself: "Undoubtedly at that place there is a distribution of food, both hard and soft. What if I were to go to where that assembly is. Perhaps there I should get some food, either hard or soft."

And the leper Suppabuddba went to where the assembly was. And the leper Suppabuddha beheld the Blessed One, surrounded by a large gathering of people, sitting and preaching the Doctrine; and when he saw the Blessed One, he said to himself: "There is no distribution here of food, either hard or soft: it is the Samana Gotama expounding the Doctrine to the people. What if I were to listen to the Doctrine?"

And be sat down there respectfully apart (saying to himself): "I, too, will listen to the Doctrine."

And the Blessed One, grasping with his own mind, the thoughts of the whole assembly, said to himself: "Who now, in this place, is able to understand the Doctrine?" And the Blessed One beheld the leper Suppabudda sitting in the midst of that assembly and when he beheld him, he said to himself: "This one is able to understand the Doctrine."

And on behalf of the leper Suppabuddha, he delivered, in regular order, the following discourses; the discourse on charity, the discourse on uprightness and the discourse on heaven, and he showed forth the worthessness and vileness of evil desires and the advantage of freedom from all the sins.

And when the Blessed One perceived that the leper Suppabuddha had a heart ready (to receive the truth), susceptible, free from hindrances, exalted and believing, he expounded to him the Doctrine as originally discovered by the Buddha and made clear to him the origin of sorrow and the way to the removal of sorrow.

Just as a pure and spotless cloth receives readily a dye, so the leper Suppabuddha, in that very place where he sat, received the pure and spotless 'Eye of the Law', namely, the knowledge that whatsoever has an origin has also an end.

And the leper Suppabuddha, perceiving the Doctrine, attaining to the Doctrine, understanding the Doctrine, sinking himself into the Doctrine, released from doubt, free from vacillation, attaining to supreme confidence in the religion of the Master, and needing nothing more, arose from his seat and went to where the Blessed One was and drawing near he saluted the

Blessed One and sat down apart, and while thus sitting he said to the Blessed One: "Excellent, Sire, Excellent Sire; it is just as if, Sire, a man should raise up that which is fallen, or discover that which is hidden, or point out the way to one who has gone astray or should bear a lamp into the darkness, so that those who have eyes may be able to see forms. Even so has the Exalted One made clear the doctrine in manifold ways. I take my refuge, Sire, in the Exalted One, in the Law and in the Brotherhood. May it please the Exalted One to receive me as his disciple; and from this day forth, as long as life lasts, I take my refuge in him."

And the leper Suppabuddha, instructed, animated, incited and gladdened by the religious discourse of the Blessed One, praised the words of the Blessed One and gave thanks. And he arose from his seat and saluted the Blessed One, and passing round keeping his right side to him, he departed. And it came to pass that the leper Suppabuddha was thrown down by a wild calf and was killed.

And a large number of Bhikkhus went to where the Blessed One was and drawing near they saluted the Blessed One and sat down respectfully apart, and while thus sitting they said to the Blessed One: "Sire, the leper Suppabuddha who was instructed, animated, incited and gladdened by the Blessed One, is now dead. What is his state, and in what condition will he be reborn?"

"A wise man, O Bhikkhus, was Suppabuddha, the leper, he practised the lesser duties for the attainment of the higher state, he did not annoy me with disputes concerning the Law--the leper Suppabuddha, O Bhikkhus, by the destruction of the three fetters, was one of those who have 'entered the stream', not subject to states of punishment, assured of salvation, having the perception of the 'four truths' as a support.

When these words had been spoken, a certain Bhikkhu said to the Blessed One: "What, Sire, was the proximate cause, what, Sire, was the concurrent cause, that the leper Suppabuddha was (in this existence) a mean, forlorn, miserable creature?"

"In a former existence, O Bhikkhus, the leper Suppabuddha was the son of a rich man in this very city of Râjagaha. While on his way through a garden, he saw the Paccekabuddha, Tagarasikhi, entering the city for alms, and when he beheld him, he said to himself: "What does this leper do walking here?" and he spat upon him and departed. He, in consequence of this action, was cast into hell for many years, for many hundreds of years, for many thousands of years, for many hundred thousands of years. In consequence of this action, he is now in this very city of Râjagaha, a mean, forlorn, miserable creature. But now by means of the discipline of the Doctrine made known by the Perfect One, he has adopted the faith, has adopted the precepts, has adopted the higher knowledge, has adopted self-sacrifice, and has adopted wisdom. He, by means of the Doctrine set forth by the Perfect One, having adopted the faith, the precepts, the higher knowledge, self-sacrifice and wisdom, on the dissolution of the body, after death, is born in the happy Kingdom of heaven, a companion of the Tavatimsa gods. There he outshines all other gods in fame and beauty."

And the Blessed One, in this connection, on that occasion, breathed forth this solemn utterance:--

*"Let him who has insight strive against existing difficulties,*
*The wise man, in the world of existence, should put evil away."*

4. Thus have I heard. On a certain occasion the Blessed One dwelt at Savatthi, in the Jetavana, the garden of Anâthapindika.

Now at that time a number of young men, between Savatthi and the Jetavana, were ill-treating some fish.

And the Blessed One, robing himself in the forenoon and taking his alms-bowl and tunic, entered Savatthi for alms. And the Blessed One beheld these young men, between Savatthi and the Jetavana, ill-treating the fish, and when he saw them, he went to where the young men were and drawing near, said to them: Young men, have you yourselves a dread of pain, is pain hateful to you?"

"Yes, Sire, we dread pain, pain is hateful to us."

And the Blessed One, in this connection, on that occasion, breathed forth this solemn utterance:--

*"If pain is hateful to you, perform no evil deed in public or in private.*
*If you should do, or do now an evil action,*
*There is no escape for you from pain, etc."*

5. Thus have I heard. On a certain occasion the Blessed One dwelt at Savatthi, in the Eastern monastery, in the pavilion of Migâramâta.

Now at that time, it being 'Uposatha' day, the Blessed One was seated, surrounded by the Brotherhood. And the venerable Ananda in the first watch of advancing night arose from his seat and adjusting his tunic upon one shoulder only (leaving the other bare), went to where the Blessed One was and stretching forth his folded hands, said to the Blessed One; "The night, Sire, is advancing, the first watch is passing, the Brethren have waited long, may it please the Blessed One to recite the canonical law to the Brethren."

When these words had been spoken, the Blessed One remained silent.

A second time the venerable Ananda, as the night advanced and the middle watch was passing, arose from his seat and adjusting his tunic upon one shoulder only, stretched forth his folded hands and said to the Blessed One: "Sire, the night is advancing, the middle watch is passing, the Brethren have waited long, may it please the Blessed One to recite the canonical law to the Brethren."

A second time the Blessed One remained silent.

A third time the venerable Ananda, in the advancing night, as the last watch was passing and dawn breaking, and the night far spent, arose from his seat and adjusting his tunic upon one shoulder only, stretched forth his folded hands and said to the Blessed One: "Sire, the night is advancing, the last watch is passing, dawn is breaking, the night is far spent, the Brethren have waited long, may it please the Blessed One to recite the canonical law to the Brethren."

"Ananda, the assembly is contaminated."

And this thought occurred to the venerable Maha Moggalana: "With reference to what individual, did the Blessed One say: 'Ananda, the assembly is contaminated'?"

And the venerable Maha Moggalana grasped with his own mind the thoughts that were in the minds of the whole of that assembly of Brethren.

And the venerable Maha Moggalana noticed an individual, in the midst of the assembly of the Brethren, who was impious, sinful by nature, of an impure, vacillating disposition, a doer of hidden deeds, not a Samana though professing Samana-ship, not living the holy life, though professing to live the holy life, foul within, full of lust, a heap of rubbish; and when he beheld him he arose from his seat and went to where that individual was and drawing near, said to him: "Arise, friend, the Blessed One has seen you, this is no place for you, here, with the Brethren."

And that person remained silent.

A second time the venerable Maha Moggallana said: "Arise, friend, the Blessed One has seen you, this is no place for you, here, with the Brethren."

A second time that person remained silent.

A third time the venerable Maha Moggallana said: "Arise, friend, the Blessed One has seen you, this is no place for you, here, with the Brethren."

A third time that person remained silent.

And the venerable Moggallana, taking him by the arm, put him outside the door of the building and having firmly closed the bolt, he went to where the Blessed One was, and drawing near said: "Sire, I have removed that person. The assembly is now free from contamination. May it please the Blessed One to recite the canonical law to the Brethren."

"How strange! Moggallana, how wonderful! That vain man will not be made to go beyond the place to which you led him by the arm."

And the Blessed One called the Bhikkhus to him and said: "From now, O Bhikkhus, and henceforth I shall not keep 'Uposatha': I shall not recite the canonical law. Do you from now, and henceforth keep 'Uposatha' and expound the precepts. This is not, O Bhikkhus, a proper occasion to explain why the Perfect One will not keep 'Uposatha': will not recite the canonical law."

"There are, O Bhikkhus, eight strange and wonderful qualities in the great ocean, perceiving which the 'Asuras' delight in the great ocean.

What are these eight?

1°. The Great Ocean, O Bhikkhus, deepens by easy gradations, by a succession of slopes, the approach to its cavernous depths is gradual, there is no sudden fall of the nature of a precipice.

As the Great Ocean, O Bhikkhus, deepens by easy gradations, [as above. *Transl.*]; This is the first strange and marvellous condition in the Great Ocean, which, when perceived by the 'Asuras', causes them to rejoice in the Great Ocean.

2°. Further, O Bhikkhus, the Great Ocean is by nature stable, it does not exceed its bounds.

Moreover, O Bhikkhus, as the Great Ocean is by nature stable and does not exceed its bounds, this is the second strange and marvellous condition which, when perceived by the 'Asuras', causes them to rejoice.

3°. Further, O Bhikkhus, the Great Ocean has no affinity with corpses, for when there are corpses in the Great Ocean, it throws them on shore, casts them on land.

Moreover, O Bhikkhus, as the Great Ocean has no affinity with corpses etc. [as above. *Transl.*]; this is the third strange and marvellous condition which, when perceived by the 'Asuras' causes them to rejoice in the Great Ocean.

4°. Further, O Bhikkhus, those large rivers, the Ganga, Yamuna, Aciravati, Mahi, when they reach the Great Ocean, abandon their ancient names and descent and are known only as the Great Ocean.

Moreover, O Bhikkhus, as those large rivers etc. etc. [as above. *Transl.*]; this is the fourth strange and marvellous condition in the Great Ocean, perceiving which the 'Asuras' rejoice in the Great Ocean.

5°. Further, O Bhikkhus, notwithstanding that all the rivers of the world and all the torrents of rain that fall from the sky, enter the Great Ocean, no deficiency or surplus of water is perceptible in the Great Ocean.

Moreover, O Bhikkhus, as, notwithstanding that all the rivers of the world etc. etc. [as above. *Transl.*]; this is the fifth strange and marvellous condition in the Great Ocean, perceiving which the 'Asuras' rejoice in the Great Ocean.

6°. Further, O Bhikkhus, the Great Ocean has one taste, the taste of salt.

And as the Great Ocean, O Bhikkhus, has but one taste, the taste of salt: This is the sixth strange and wonderful condition, perceiving which the 'Asuras' rejoice in the Great Ocean.

7°. Further, O Bhikkhus, the Great Ocean is full of gems and precious things of great variety, such as, pearls, emeralds, lapis lazuli, shells, stones, coral, silver, gold, rubies and cats-eyes.

As, O Bhikkhus, the Great Ocean is full of gems etc. [as above. *Transl.*]; this is the seventh strange and marvellous condition, perceiving which the 'Asuras' rejoice in the Great Ocean.

8°. Further, O Bhikkhus, the Great Ocean is the abode of a multitude of living creatures; namely, all those monstrous fish which haunt the oceans between the 'Seven Mountains', the Tritons, the Serpent Kings, the Celestial Musicians and creatures that are one, two, three, four and five hundred leagues in length.

And as, O Bhikkhus, the Great Ocean is the abode of a multitude of living creatures etc. [as above. *Transl.*]; this is the eighth strange and marvellous condition, perceiving which the 'Asuras' rejoice in the Great Ocean.

Even so, O Bhikkhus, in the discipline of the Law, there are eight wonderful and astonishing conditions perceiving which, the Bhikkhus rejoice in the discipline of the Law.

What are these eight?

1°. Just as the Great Ocean, O Bhikkhus, deepens by easy gradations, by a succession of slopes, and the approach to its cavernous depths is gradual, and there is no sudden fall in the nature of a precipice, even so, O Bhikkhus, is the discipline of the Law. The training is gradual, there is a regular succession of duties, progress is made step by step; there is no sudden penetration into the higher wisdom. This is the first marvellous and astonishing condition in the discipline of the Law, perceiving which the Bhikkhus rejoice in the discipline of the Law.

2°. Just as the Great Ocean, O Bhikkhus, is by nature stable and does not exceed its bounds, even so, O Bhikkhus, my disciples, even for the sake of continued existence, do not exceed the precepts ordained by me for the disciples.

This is the second strange and marvellous condition in the discipline of the Law, perceiving which the Bhikkhus rejoice in the discipline of the Law.

3°. Just as the Great Ocean, O Bhikkhus, has no affinity with corpses, and when there is a corpse in the Great Ocean, it casts it on shore and throws it on land, even so, O Bhikkhus, the Brotherhood has no affinity with a man who is impious, evil by nature, impure, vacillating, doing hidden deeds, professing to be a Samana and is not a Samana, professing to be a Brahmana and is not a Brahmana, foul within, full of lust, a heap of rubbish--such a one, when the Assembly meets, it soon ejects. If such a one sits in the midst of the Assembly he is far from that Assembly and the Assembly from him.

As, O Bhikkhus a man who is impious [as above *Transl.*] etc. is far from that Assembly and the Assembly from him; this is the third strange and astonishing condition in the discipline of the Law, perceiving which the Bhikkhus rejoice in the discipline of the Law.

4°. Just as, O Bhikkhus, the great rivers, the Ganga, Yamuna, Acirivati, Sarabhu, Mahi, when they reach the Great Ocean, abandon their old names and old descent, and bear only one name 'the Great Ocean', even so O Bhikkhus, the four castes, Khattiyas, Brahmanas, Vessas, Suddas, in accordance with the discipline of the Law taught by the Perfect One, forsake their homes for the home-less state, leave behind them their old names and old descent, and are called Samanas, sons of the Sâkiya race.

As, O Bhikkhus the four castes etc. [as above. *Transl.*] are called Samanas, sons of the Sakya race, this is the fourth strange and marvellous condition in the discipline of the Law, perceiving which the Bhikkhus rejoice in the discipline of the Law.

5°. Just as, O Bhikkhus, (notwithstanding that all the rivers in the world and all the torrents of rain that fall from the sky flow into the Great Ocean) there is no deficiency or surplus of water perceptible in the Great Ocean, even so, O Bhikkhus, if innumerable Bhikkhus attain to that extinction of 'becoming', through the element of Nirvana in which no trace of the attributes of 'becoming' remains, there is no diminution or surplus perceptible in the element of Nirvana.

As, O Bhikkhus, innumerable Bhikkhus [as above. *Transl.*] etc. there is no diminution or surplus perceptible in the element of Nirvana; this is the fifth strange and marvellous condition, O Bhikkhus, perceiving which the Bhikkhus rejoice in the discipline of the Law.

6°. Just as, O Bhikkhus, the Great Ocean has but one taste, the taste of salt, even so, O Bhikkhus, this doctrine has but one taste, the taste of Deliverance; and as, O Bhikkhus, this doctrine has but one taste, the taste of deliverance; this is the sixth stange and marvellous condition in the discipline of the Law perceiving which the Bhikkhus rejoice in the discipline of the Law.

7°. Just as the Great Ocean, O Bhikkhus, is full of many gems, etc. [as above. *Transl.*], even so, O Bhikkhus, this Doctrine is full of many gems and precious things; the four 'Earnest Meditations' and 'Great Exertions', the four 'Constituents of Superhuman power', the five 'Moral Qualities', the five 'Forces', the five 'Constituents of Supreme Knowledge', and the 'Noble Eight-fold Path'.

And as this doctrine is full of many gems etc. [as above. *Transl.*] and the 'Noble Eight-fold Path'; this is the seventh strange and wonderful condition in the discipline of the Law, perceiving which the Bhikkhus rejoice in the discipline of the Law.

8°. Just as the Great Ocean, O Bhikkhus, is the abode of many living creatures etc. [as above. *Transl.*] even so, O Bhikkhus, in this dicipline of the Law there are many members, the Sotapanna who has attained to a realization of the fruition of a Sotapanna, the Sakadâgamini who has attained to a realization of the fruition of a Sakadâgamini, the Anâgamini

47

who has attained to a realization of the fruition of an Anâgamini, the Arahat who has attained to Arahatship.

And as, O Bhikkhus, in this discipline of the Law there are many members etc. [as above. *Transl.*] this is the eighth condition in the discipline of the Law, perceiving which the Bhikkhus rejoice in the discipline of the Law. These, O Bhikkhus, are the eight strange and marvellous conditions in the discipline of the Law, perceiving which the Bhikkhus rejoice therein."

And the Blessed One, in this connection, on that occasion, breathed forth this solemn utterance:--

*"The rain pours down upon the well-roofed house*
*It falls not upon the house that is roofless,*
*Therefore open wide that which is closed,*
*And the rain will not descend upon it."*

6. Thus have I heard. On a certain occasion the Blessed One dwelt at Savatthi, in the Jetavana, the garden of Anâthapindika.

Now at that time the venerable Mahakaccana was living in the Avanti country, on the hill called the Precipice, in Kuraraghara, And at that time the lay-disciple Sona Kotikanna was the servitor of the venerable Mahakaccana.

While enjoying the bliss of solitude, this thought arose in the mind of the lay-disciple Sona Kotikanna: "According to the doctrine taught by the venerable Mahakaccana it is not easy for the man who dwells at home, to live the higher life, in entire fulfilment, in complete purity, in all its bright perfection. What if I were to shave my head and beard, assume the yellow robe, and go forth from my home into the state of homelessness."

And the lay-disciple Sona Kotikanna went to where the venerable Mahakaccana was and drawing near, he saluted the venerable Mahakaccana and sat down apart, and while thus sitting he said to the venerable Mahakaccana: "Just now, Sire, as I was enjoying the bliss of solitude, this thought arose in my mind: "According to the doctrine etc. [as above. *Transl.*]."

"May it please the Lord Mahakaccana to receive me into the Order of those who have renounced the world."

When these words had been spoken, the venerable Mahakaccana said to the lay-disciple Sona Kotikanna: "Hard is it, O Sona, to live for a life-time the higher life, to partake of one meal a day, to sleep apart. I pray you, Sona, to remain for the present in the condition of a housholder, while practising the precepts of the Buddhas, and partaking of one meal a day and sleeping apart."

And the fancy which the lay-disciple Sona Kotikanna had for the ascetic life, subsided.

A second time, as the lay-disciple Sona Kotikanna was enjoying the bliss of solitude, this thought arose: "According to the doctrine etc. [as above.

*Transl.*]: "What if I were to etc. [as above. *Transl.*] and go forth from my home into the homeless state."

A second time the venerable Mahakaccana said: "Hard is it, O Sona, etc. [as above. *Transl.*]."

A third time, as the lay-disciple Sona Kotikanna was enjoying the bliss etc. [as above. *Transl.*].

"May it please the Lord Mahakaccana to receive me into the Order of those who have renounced the world."

And the venerable Mahakaccana received the lay-disciple Sana Kotikanna into the Order of those who have renaunced the world.

Now at that time there were very few monks in the Southern districts of the Avanti country.

At the end of three years, the venerable Mahakaccana with difficulty and trouble, collecting monks from here and there, managed to form a Chapter of ten monks. And the venerable Sona was admitted into the higher ranks of the Order.

As the venerable Sona was passing the rainy season in solitude, there occurred to him the thought: "I have not seen the Blessed One, face to face, but I have heard he is such and such. If my teacher approves, I will go and see the Exalted One, that Saint, the Supreme Buddha."

And the venerable Sona, arising at eventide from his solitary communing, went to where the venerable Mahakaccana was and drawing near saluted him and sat down apart and while thus sitting the venerable Sona said to him: "Just now, Sire, while passing the rainy season in solitude, this thought occurred to me: "I have not seen the Blessed one [as above. *Transl.*] I will go and see . . . the Supreme Buddha."

"It is well, Sona, it is well; go and see the Exalted One, that Saint, the Supreme Buddha. You will behold the holy, the Gracious One, the dispenser of joy, whose senses are placid, whose spirit is at rest; who has attained to supreme self-conquest,--the hero, the subdued, the Guarded One, whose desires are stilled; and when you behold him, in my name, bow down in salutation at his feet and say: "My master, Sire, the venerable Mahakaccana bows his head in salutation at the feet of the Exalted One and asks, 'if there is any slight ailment, if there is freedom from bodily fatigue, if he is vigorous, strong and in good health'.""

"Be it so," said the venerable Sona and praising the words spoken by the venerable Mahakaccana, and giving thanks, he put his sleeping place in order, and taking his alms-bowl and tunic departed on his way to Savatthi. And wandering from place to place he came to the Jetavana, the garden of Anâthapindika, at Savatthi where the Blessed One dwelt and drawing near he saluted the Blessed One and sat down apart and while thus sitting he said to the Blessed One: "My Master enquires if there is any slight ailment etc. [as above. *Transl.*].

"I trust, O Bhikkhu, (said the Blessed One) that it is well with you, that you are able to support life, that you have performed your journey with little fatigue, that you have not been wearied in quest of alms."

"It is well with me, Exalted One, I am able to support life, I have performed the journey with little fatigue, I have not wearied myself in quest of alms."

And the Blessed One called the venerable Ananda to him and said: "Prepare, Ananda, a sleeping place for this newly arrived Bhikkhu."

And it occurred to the venerable Ananda: "Since the Blessed One has commanded me to prepare a sleeping place for this newly arrived Bhikkhu, the Blessed One desires to live alone with the venerable Sona"; and he prepared a sleeping place for the venerable Sona in the monastery which the Blessed One occupied. And the Blessed One having spent the greater part of the night sitting in the open air, washed his feet and entered the monastery. And the venerable Sona having spent the greater part of the night in the open air, washed his feet and entered the monastery. And the Blessed One arising in the morning, called the venerable Sona to him and said: "May the Doctrine become so clear that you may recite it to the Bhikkhus."

"Be it so", said the venerable Sona in assent to the Blessed One, and he intoned all the sixteen chapters of the 'Atthaka'.

And the Blessed One, at the conclusion of the venerable Sona's recitation, expressed his delight, saying: "Excellent, O Bhikkhu, excellent! Those sixteen chapters of the 'Atthaka' have been well grasped, thoroughly thought out, and understood: you are gifted with a sweet voice, distinct and faultless, and are able to explain the meaning of things. How many years have you been ordained?"

"One year, Sire."

"Why, O Bhikkhu, did you delay it so long?"

"For a long time, Sire, I have seen the worthlessness of desire; moreover the housholder's life is crowded with business and many anxieties."

And the Blessed One, in this connection, on that occasion, breathed forth this solemn utterance:

*"He who has seen the evils of a wordly life,*
*Who has understood the Truth, and is free from Upadhi,*
*He who has entered the Path, delights not in Evil,*
*The Pure in heart finds no pleasure in Sin."*

7. Thus have I heard. On a certain occasion the Blessed One dwelt at Savatthi, in the Jetavana, the garden of Anâthapindika.

Now at that time the venerable Kankharevata was sitting, not far from the Blessed One, in a cross-legged position, with body erect, contemplating his state of purity and deliverance from doubt.

And the Blessed One beheld the venerable Kankharevata, sitting near, in a cross-legged position, with body erect, contemplating his state of purity and deliverance from doubt.

And the Blessed One, in this connection, on that occasion, breathed forth this solemn utterance:

*"All those meditative, ardent Saints doubt,*
*Either in this world or the next,*
*Whether expressed by themselves or others,*
*They are those who live the higher life."*

8. Thus have I heard. On a certain occasion the Blessed One dwelt at Râjagaha, in the Bambu Grove, in Kalandakanivapa.

Now at that time the venerable Ananda, it being Uposatha day, robed himself in the forenoon and taking his alms-bowl and tunic, entered Râjagaha for alms.

And Devadatta beheld the venerable Ananda going his rounds for alms in Râjagaha and when he saw him he went to where the venerable Anânda was and drawing near, said to him: "Henceforth from to day I shall keep Uposatha day and carry out the work of the Sangha without reference to the Blessed One or to the Brotherhood."

And the venerable Ananda having gone his rounds in Râjagaha and finished his meal went to where the Blessed One was and drawing near he saluted the Blessed One and sat down apart, and while thus sitting he said to the Blessed One: "Just now, Sire, having robed myself in the forenoon and taking my alms-bowl and tunic, I entered Râjagaha for alms.

And Devadatta when he saw me going my rounds in Râjagaha came to me and said: "Henceforth from to-day I shall keep Uposatha day etc. [as above. *Transl.*].

To-day, Sire, Devadatta will break up the Assembly and keep Uposatha day and carry on the work of the Assembly by himself."

And the Blessed One, in this connection, on that occasion, breathed forth this solemn utterance:

*"It is easy for the good to do good,*
*It is hard for the good to do evil,*
*It is easy for the evil to do evil*
*It is hard for the Saint to do evil."*

9. Thus have I heard. On a certain occasion the Blessed One, in company with a large following of the Brethren, was wandering apart in the Kosala country.

Now at that time a number of youths not far from the Blessed One were creating a great uproar. And the Blessed One beheld these youths creating a great uproar.

And the Blessed One in this connection, on that occasion breathed forth this solemn utterance:

51

"Bewildered are the clever words of him who is versed in the resources of eloquence. As wide as they like they open their mouths. By whom led they know not."

10. Thus have I heard. On a certain occasion the Blessed One dwelt at Savatthi, in the Jetavana, the garden of Anâthapindika.

Now at that time the venerable Culapanthaka was sitting, not far from the Blessed One, in a cross-legged position, with body erect, placing memory directly before him.

And the Blessed One beheld the venerable Culapanthaka sitting, not far off, in a cross-legged position, with body erect, placing memory directly before him.

And the Blessed One, in this connection, on that occasion, breathed forth this solemn utterance:

*"The Bhikkhu who, whether standing or sitting or lying down,*
*Thus concentrates his attention on memory, with body and mind intent,*
*Such a one will obtain the 'successive advantages.'*
*And he who obtains the 'successive advantages'*
*Will not be seen of the King of Death."*

# CHAPTER VI. JACCANDHA.

1. Thus have I heard. On a certain occasion the Blessed One dwelt at Vesali, in the Mahavana, in the Pagoda Hall.

And the Blessed One, having robed himself in the forenoon, and taking his alms-bowl and tunic entered Vesali for alms. And when he had returned from his rounds and finished his meal, he called the venerable Ananda to him and said: "Take up, Ananda, the mat, I will pass the heat of the day at the Câpâla shrine."

"Be it so, Sire" said the venerable Ananda in assent to the Blessed One, and taking up the mat, he followed the Blessed One step by step.

And the Blessed One went to where the Câpâla shrine was, and drawing near, he sat down on the appointed seat, and while thus sitting he called the venerable Ananda to him and said: "Delightful, Ananda, is the Gotamaka shrine, delightful is the Sattamba shrine, delightful is the Bahuputta shrine, delightful is the Sarandada shrine, delightful is the Câpâla shrine! Whoever, Ananda, has dwelt upon, enlarged, made use of as a vehicle, objectified, taken as a foundation, amalgamated, and most thoroughly striven with the constituents of magic power, if he should so wish, is able to remain in this world a Kalpa, or the remainder of a Kalpa. The Perfect One, Ananda, has dwelt upon, enlarged, made use of as a vehicle, objectified, taken as a foundation, amalgamated, and most thoroughly striven with the constituents of magic power, and if he so wish, can remain in this world a Kalpa, or the remainder of a Kalpa."

And the venerable Ananda failing to penetrate the meaning of the palpable sign made and the clear hint given by the Blessed One, did not beseech the Blessed One and say: "May it please the Blessed One to remain in this world a Kalpa, may it please the Happy One to remain a Kalpa for the welfare of many, for the happiness of many, in compassion for the people, for the benefit, the advantage, the delight of men and gods--so possessed was the heart of Ananda by the Wicked One.

A second time the Blessed One called the venerable Ananda to him and said etc. (repetition as above. *Transl.*].

A third time etc. [repetition as above *Transl.*]

And the Blessed One called the venerable Ananda to him and said: "Go now, Ananda, and do as you like."

"Be it so, Sire," said the venerable Ananda in assent to the Blessed One and rising from his seat, he saluted the Blessed One, and passing round keeping his right side to him, he went and sat down, not far off, at the foot of a tree.

And soon after the departure of the venerable Ananda, Mâra, the Evil One, came to where the Blessed One was, and drawing near, he stood respectfully apart and while thus standing Mâra the Evil One said to the Blessed One: "Pass away now, Exalted One, let the Happy One now die:

now is the time for the Exalted One to pass away from existence, for the Exalted One has spoken these words: 'I shall not pass away from existence, thou Wicked One, until I shall have gained monks as my disciples, who are wise and disciplined, well trained, secure in the Doctrine, erudite, versed in the Law, experts in the higher and lower doctrines, correct in their conduct, practised in the lesser duties, to proclaim, teach, make known, elucidate, analyze, and make clear what they have learned from their Master, to refute and demolish by their knowledge any defamation of the doctrine, and to spread the wonder-working truth abroad'. Now, Sire, the Exalted One has gained monks as disciples who are wise and disciplined etc. [as above. *Transl.*]: Pass away now, Exalted One, from existence: let the Happy One now die: now is the time for the Exalted One to pass away from existence. And the Exalted One, moreover has spoken these words: 'I shall not pass away from existence, thou Wicked One, until I have gained nuns as my disciples. [repetition as above. *Transl.*].

Until I have gained male votaries etc. d°. d°.

Until I have gained female votaries etc. d°. d°.'

The Exalted One moreover has said: 'I shall not pass away from existence, thou Wicked One, until the 'holy life' is successful, prosperous, wide-spread among all sections of humanity, and thoroughly made manifest to gods and men.' Now, Sire, the 'holy life' spoken of by the Exalted One, is successful, prosperous, wide-spread among all sections of humanity, and thoroughly made manifest to gods and men. Pass away now from existence, Exalted One, let the Happy One now die, now is the time for the Exalted One to enter into Nirvana."

When these words had been spoken, the Blessed One said to Mâra, the Evil One: "Be not anxious, thou Wicked One; soon will the Perfect One pass away from existence: three months hence the Perfect One will enter Nirvana."

And the Blessed One, there in the Câpâla shrine, mindful and conscious, relinquished the natural term of life, and when the Blessed One relinquished the natural term of life, the earth quaked, and thunder, horror-fraught and terrible, burst forth from heaven.

And the Blessed One, in this connection, on that occasion, breathed forth this solemn utterance:

*"The Sage renounced his life, the cause of life, both long and short.*
*With inward calm and joy, he broke, like coat of mail, his life's own cause."*

2. Thus have I heard. On a certain occasion the Blessed One dwelt at Savatthi, in the Eastern monastery, in the pavilion of Migaramâta.

Now at that time, the Blessed One, having arisen at eventide from his solitary communings was sitting outside in the portico.

And the King Pasenadi Kosala went to where the Blessed One was and drawing near saluted the Blessed One and sat down respectfully apart.

Now at that time, seven ascetics with long matted hair, seven Niganthas, seven Acelas, seven wearing only one garment, and seven wandering monks with overgrown nails and hair, carrying with them various requisites of monks, were passing by, not far from the Blessed One.

And when the King Pasenadi Kosala beheld these seven ascetics, etc. [as above. *Transl.*] passing by close to the Blessed One, he arose from his seat and placing his upper robe upon one shoulder only (leaving the other bare), he knelt with his right knee on the ground and clasping his hands, three times proclaimed his name to the ascetics: "I am, reverend Sirs, the King Pasenadi Kosala."

Soon after the departure of the ascetics, the King Pasenadi Kosala went to where the Blessed One was and drawing near he saluted the Blessed One and sat down apart and while thus sitting the King Pasenadi Kosala said to the Blessed One: "Are these ascetics, Sire, among those who are reckoned in this world as saints, or as having entered the path that leads to Saintship?"

"Hard is it, Great King, for you, in the enjoyment of a housholder's life, living surrounded by sons, using the powder of sandal wood from Benares, wearing perfumed garlands and in the possession of gold and silver, to tell if these ascetics are saints or on the path that leads to Saintship. Only by living with them, Great King, for a long time, can their virtues be ascertained and this requires much reflection, thought, wisdom and knowledge. Only by associating, Great King, for a long time with them in their modes of life can their integrity be ascertained, and this requires [as above.]. etc. Only by associating with them, Great King, for a long time in their troubles can their persistence be ascertained, and this requires etc. [as above].

Only by conversing with them, Great King, for a long time can their wisdom be ascertained, and this requires much reflection, thought, wisdom and knowledge."

"Wonderful, Sire, marvellous are the words so well spoken by the Blessed One: 'Hard is it, etc. [as above].'"

There are, Sire, certain of my people going about the country, who may be likened to robbers, for they receive alms without having renounced the world. When these have entered the 'path', I will do likewise. As yet, Sire, these people have not removed the dust-heap (of desire), and go about, anointed with oil; with head and beard shorn, in white garments, possessed of and endowed with the 'five pleasures of sense'."

And the Blessed One, in this connection, on that occasion, breathed forth this solemn utterance:

*"Should a man not exert himself on every occasion, not exist for another,*
*Not live for the sake of others,*
*Truly, he does not live the holy life".*

3. Thus have I heard. On a certain occasion the Blessed One dwelt at Savatthi, in the Jetavana, the garden of Anâthapindika.

Now at that time the Blessed One was sitting, looking back upon the various evil and wicked conditions abandoned by him, and contemplating the many good conditions fulfilled.

And the Blessed One looking back upon the various evil and wicked conditions abandoned by him and contemplating the many good conditions fulfilled, on that occasion, breathed forth this solemn utterance:

*"That which was, is not now: that which was not formerly, now is:*
*It has not been, it will not be, it is not now."*

4. Thus have I heard. On a certain occasion, the Blessed One dwelt at Savatthi, in the Jetavana, the garden of Anâthapindika.

Now at that time a large number of Samanas, Brahmanas and wandering monks of various heretical sects, holding a variety of views, doubters on many points, having many diverse aspirations, and recourse to that which relates to various heresies, entered Savatthi for alms.

Some of these Samanas and Brahmanas held that the world is eternal and contended that this view was true and every other false.

Some said: the world is not eternal.

Some said: the world is finite.

Some said: the world is infinite.

Some said: the soul and the body are identical.

Some said: the soul and the body are not identical.

Some said: the Perfect One continues to exist after death.

Some said: The Perfect One does not continue to exist after death.

Some said: The Perfect One exists and does not exist after death.

Some said: The Perfect One neither exists nor does not exist after death.

Each contending their view was true and every other false.

These quarrelsome, pugnacious, cavilling monks wounded one another with sharp words (lit. mouth-javelins) declaiming: "such is the truth, such is not the truth: the truth is not such, such is the truth."

And a number of Bhikkhus, robing themselves in the forenoon and taking their alms-bowls and tunics, entered Savatthi for alms and when they had returned from their rounds and finished their meal, they went to where the Blessed One was and drawing near, they saluted the Blessed One and sat down apart, and while thus sitting they said to the Blessed One: "Just now, Sire, a large number of Samanas and Brahmanas and wandering monks holding varions heresies entered Savatthi for alms, and they are disputing among themselves, saying: '"This is the truth, such is not the truth etc. [as above. *Transl.*]"

"These heretical monks, O Bhikkhus, are blind, eyeless, they know not what is right, they know not what is wrong, they know not what is true, they know not what is false. These monks not perceiving what is right, not perceiving what is wrong, not perceiving what is true, not perceiving what is false, become disputations, saying: 'such is the truth, such is not the truth' etc. [as above. *Transl.*]

In former times, O Bhikkhus, there was a King in this town of Savatthi. And the King, O Bhikkhus, called a man to him and said: "Go, thou, and collect all the men born blind in Savatthi and bring them here."

"Be it so, Lord" said that man in assent to the King and he went to Savatthi and he brought all the men born blind in Savatthi to where the King was and drawing near he said to the King: "Lord, all the men blind from their birth in Savatthi are present."

"Pray, then, bring an elephant before them."

"Be it so, Lord" said that man in assent to the King and he brought an elephant into the presence of the blind men and said: "This, O blind men, is an elephant."

To some of the blind men he presented the head of the elephant, saying, 'Such, O blind men, is an elephant.'

To some he presented the body, saying: 'such is an elephant.'

To some he presented the feet, saying: 'Such is an elephant.'

To some he presented the back, saying: 'Such is an elephant.'

To some he presented the tail, saying: 'Such is an elephant.'

To some he presented the hairy tuft of the tail, saying: 'Such is an elephant.'

The show-man, O Bhikkhus, having presented the elephant to these blind ones, went to where the King was and drawing near said to the King: "The elephant, Lord, has been brought before the blind men, do now as seems fit."

And the King went to where the blind men were, and drawing near said to them: "Do you now know what an elephant is like?"

"Assuredly, Lord: we now know what an elephant is like."

"Tell me then, O blind men, what an elephant is like."

And those blind men, O Bhikkhus, who had felt the head of the elephant, said: 'An elephant, Sir, is like a large round jar .

Those who had felt its ears, said: 'it is like a winnowing basket.'

Those who had felt its tusks, said: 'it is like a plough-share.'

Those who had felt its trunk, said: 'it is like a plough.'

Those who had felt its body, said: 'it is like a granary:

Those who had felt its feet, said: 'it is like a pillar.'

Those who had felt its back, said: 'it is like a mortar.'

Those who had felt its tail, said: 'it is a like a pestle.'

Those who had felt the tuft of its tail, said: 'it is like a broom.'

And they all fought amongst themselves with their fists, declaring, 'such is an elephant, such is not elephant, an elephant is not like that, it is like this.'

And the King, O Bhikkhus, was highly delighted.

In exactly the same way, O Bhikkhus, do these heretical people, blind and without insight, dispute among themselves saying 'this doctrine is true, every other is false'."

And the Blessed One in this connection, on that occasion, breathed forth this solemn utterance:

*"Well is it known that some Samanas and Brahmanas,*
*Who attach themselves to methods of analysis,*
*And perceiving only one side of a case,*
*Disagree with one another."*

5. Thus have I heard. On a certain occasion the Blessed One dwelt at Savatthi, in the Jetavana, the garden of Anâthapindika.

Now at that time a great number of wandering monks, Samanas and Brahmanas, belonging to various heretical sects, holding a variety of views, doubters on many points, with diverse aspirations and having recourse to that which relates to diverse heresies, entered Savatthi for alms.

These Samanas and Brahmanas held various views, such as:

The self and the world are eternal.

The self and the world are both finite and infinite.

The self and the world are neither finite nor infinite.

The self and the world are self-produced.

The self and the world are both self-produced and other-produced.

The self and the world are neither self-produced nor other-produced.

The self and the world spring into existence without a cause.

The self and the world, ease and discomfort are eternal.

The self and the world, ease and discomfort, are not eternal.

(The above) are both finite and infinite.

(The above) are self-produced.

(The above) are other-produced.

(The above) are both self-produced and other-produced.

(The above) are both not self-produced and not other-produced, nor have they sprung into existence without a cause.

Thus they disagreed, each one declaring 'this view is true, every other false.'

And a number of Bhikkhus etc. went to where the Blessed One was and said: 'Just now, Sire, a number of Samanas and Brahmanas etc. [as before. *Transl.*] saying 'this view is true, every other false.'

"These wandering monks, O Bhikkhus, blind, without insight, belonging to various heretical sects, perceive not what is right nor what is wrong, know not what is true, nor what is false, and perceiving not what is right or what is wrong and knowing not what is true or what is false, dispute among themselves, saying etc. [as above. *Transl*].

And the Blessed One, in this connection, on that occasion, breathed forth this solemn utterance:

*"Well it is known that some Samanas and Brahmanas,*
*Cling to such views, sink down into them,*
*And attain not to Nirvana."*

6. *The same as above but with the following ending.*

"This people are possessed with the notions, 'I am the doer,' 'another is the doer.' They do not understand (that these are two heresies). They see no harm in them. He who perceives the harm in them, does not entertain the ideas, 'I am the doer', 'another is the doer.'

This people, given to pride, stubborn in pride, in bondage to pride, clamourous in heretical talk, pass not beyond the Ocean of birth and death."

7. Thus have I heard. On a certain occasion the Blessed One dwelt at Savatthi, in the Jetavana, the garden of Anâthapindika.

Now at that time the venerable Subhuti was sitting not far from the Blessed One, in a cross-legged position, with body erect, having entered into a state of thoughtless trance. And the Blessed One saw the venerable Subhuti sitting, not far off in a cross-legged position, with body erect, having entered into a state of thoughtless trance.

And the Blessed One, in this connection, on that occasion, breathed forth this solemn utterance:

*"He by whom evil thought is destroyed,*
*And every inward reflection is well considered,*
*He, unconscious of corporeal form, passing beyond 'attachment,'*
*Overcoming the 'four fetters', is not reborn."*

8. Thus have I heard. On a certain occasion the Blessed One dwelt at Râjagaha, in the Bamboo Grove, in Kalandikanivapa.

Now at that time there were two men of Râjagaha deeply enamoured of and in love with a certain courtezan.

They quarrelled, argued and disputed, and attacked each other with trowels, with clods of earth, with sticks and with swords. In this cause they were prepared to face death and the pangs of death.

And a large number of Bhikkhus, robing themselves in the forenoon and taking their alms-bowls and tunics entered Râjagaha for alms and when they had gone their rounds in Râjagaha and finished their meal, they went to where the Blessed One was, and drawing near, they saluted the Blessed One and sat down apart and while thus sitting they said to him: "Just now, Sire, two men of Râjagaha, deeply enamoured of and in love with a certain courtezan etc. [as above. *Transl.*]."

And the Blessed One, in this connection, on that occasion, breathed forth this solemn utterance:

"There are those that hold as essential truth the teaching of him who is an inculcator of trouble [of the view that] whatever one has attanied, or is to attain is sprinkled over with evil. There are those who accept as helps morality, good life, chastity. This is the one ideal [the aim] of him who argues thus.

And there is a second ideal: to wit, that there is no harm in lusts. Both these ideals of life--that of despair of good, and that of the sensualist-- enlarge the realm of death, and that [in its turn] tends to the increase of speculation. Some, not understanding [the real nature of] these ideals, stick to them, some get beyond them. Those who see through them, are not in them, do not think that way, their revolution is beyond perception [that is, they do not revolve in Samsara, they attain Nirvana in this life and are not subject to rebirths and redeaths."]

9. Thus have I heard. On a certain occasion the Blessed One dwelt at Savatthi, in the Jetavana, the garden of Anâthapindika.

Now at that time the Blessed One, was sitting in the open air, the night was profoundly dark and oil-lamps were alight.

And a number of moths falling over and over into these oil-lamps, met with disaster, ruin and utter destruction. And the Blessed One beheld these moths falling over and over into the oil-lamps, meeting with disaster, ruin and utter destruction.

And the Blessed One, in this connection, on that occasion, breathed forth this solemn utterance:

*"They run up to it and beyond,*
*But never reach the essence.*
*They magnify to themselves new and ever new bonds.*
*As the moths fall into the flame,*
*So, some are attracted [by the doctrine]*
*That, in the seen and the heard [is the essence]."*

10. Thus have I heard. On a certain occasion the Blessed One dwelt at Savatthi, in the Jetavana, the garden of Anâthapindika.

And the venerable Ananda went to where the Blessed One was and having saluted him, sat down apart, and while thus sitting, the venerable Ananda said to the Blessed One: "Until, Sire, the Perfect Ones, the Saints, the Supreme Buddhas are born in the world, the heretical sects and wandering monks are held in honour, worshipped, esteemed and reverenced, and are recipients of the requisites of monks, such as, robes, alms, sleeping places, and drugs in case of sickness, but when the Perfect Ones, the Saints, the Supreme Buddhas appear on earth then these heretical sects and wandering monks are not held in honour, worshipped, esteemed and reverenced and are not recipients of the requisites of monks, such as, robes, alms, sleeping places and drugs in case of sickness. Now, Sire, the

Blessed One and the Brotherhood are held in honour etc. and are recipients of etc. and drugs in case of sickness."

"It is so, Ananda; until the Perfect Ones, the Saints, the Supreme Buddhas etc. the heretical sects etc. are recipients of the requisites etc."

And the Blessed One, in this connection, on that occasion, breathed forth this solemn utterance:

*"The light of the glowworm is seen, until the rising of the sun;*
*In the splendour of the sun-rise, its light fades and shines no more.*
*So is it with the light of the heretics.*
*Until the Supreme Buddhas appear on earth:*
*Not till then do the wise and the disciples receive enlightenment.*
*Those who hold heretical views, escape not from sorrow."*

# CHAPTER VII. CULA.

1. Thus have I heard. On a certain occasion the Blessed One dwelt at Savatthi, in the Jetavana, the garden of Anâthapindika.

Now at that time the venerable Sâriputta was instructing, arousing, animating and gladdening the venerable Dwarf Bhaddiya with manifold religious discourses.

And thus instructed, aroused, animated and gladdened by the mainfold religions discourses of the venerable Sariputta, the heart of the venerable Dwarf Bhaddiya was set free from 'attachment' and the sins.

And the Blessed One perceived that the heart of the venerable Bhaddiya was set free from 'attachment' and the sins, through the manifold religious discourses of the venerable Sâriputta.

And the Blessed One, in this connection, on that occasion, breathed forth this solemn utterance:

*"Above, below, in every respect emancipated,*
*Perceiving that there is no 'Ego',*
*Such a one, free, has crossed the flood, not crossed before,*
*And is reborn no more."*

2. Thus have I heard. At that time the Blessed One dwelt at Savatthi, in the Jetavana, the garden of Anâthapindika.

And the venerable Sâriputta thinking that the venerable Dwarf Bhaddiya was yet but a novice, instructed, aroused, animated and gladdened him with manifold religious discourses.

And the Blessed One perceived the venerable Sâriputta instructing, arousing, animating and gladdening the venerable Dwarf Bhaddiya (whom he thought yet a novice) with manifold religious discourses.

And the Blessed One, in this connection, on that occasion breathed forth this solemn utterance:

*"The wheel is broken. The 'desire-less' attained.*
*The river bed is dry, no water flows,*
*No more the broken wheel will roll;*
*This is the end of sorrow".*

3. Thus have I heard. On a certain occasion the Blessed One dwelt at Savatthi, in the Jetavana, the garden of Anâthapindika.

Now at that time a number of men were living at Savatthi and all of them were in bondage to the passions, inflamed, glutted, seized and infatuated to excess with lust, falling into sin and impregnated with lust.

And a number of Bhikkhus, robing themselves in the forenoon and taking their alms-bowls and tunics entered Savatthi for alms, and when they had returned from their rounds in Savatthi and finished their meal, they went to where the Blessed One was, and drawing near, they saluted the Blessed One and sat down apart and while thus sitting they said to the

Blessed One: "at this time, Sire, a number of men are passing their days in Savatthi, in bondage to the passions etc. [as above. *Transl.*]."

And the Blessed One in this connection, on that occasion, breathed forth this solemn utterance:

*"These are beings inflamed with lust,*
*Bound in the bonds of passion,*
*Who perceive no evil in the 'fetters'.*
*Verily these who are bound by the fetters of human passion,*
*Cross not the great and mighty flood*
*(of evil which overwhelms humanity.)"*

4. Thus have I heard. On a certain occasion the Blessed One dwelt at Savatthi, in the Jetavana, the garden of Anâthapindika.

At that time a number of men were living at Savatthi, and all of them were in bondage to the passions, inflamed, glutted, seized and infatuated to excess with lust, falling into sin, blinded and impregnated with lust.

And the Blessed One, robing himself in the forenoon and taking his alms-bowl and tunic entered Savatthi for alms.

And the Blessed One beheld these men living at Savatthi and all of them in bondage to the passions, inflamed etc. [as above. *Transl.*].

And the Blessed One, in this connection, on that occasion, breathed forth this solemn utterance:

*"These people blinded with lust, entangled,*
*Clothed in the garments of desire,*
*Imprisoned in the bonds of indolence--*
*Like fish in a funnel-shaped net--*
*They hasten onwards to decay and death,*
*As a sucking calf to its mother."*

5. Thus have I heard, On a certain occasion the Blessed One dwelt at Savatthi, in the Jetavana, the garden of Anâthapindika.

Now at that time the venerable dwarf Bhaddiya, following step by step in the wake of a large number of Bhikkhus, came to where the Blessed One was.

And when the Blessed One beheld the venerable dwarf Bhaddiya, coming along in the wake of the Bhikkhus, ill-favored, evil to behold, lowly in gait and despised by the majority of the Bhikkhus, he called the Bhikkhus to him and said: "Behold, O Bhikkhus, this mendicant approaching from afar, ill-favored, evil to behold, lowly in gait, and despised by the majority of Bhikkhus,"

"Even so, Sire."

"This mendicant, O Bhikkhus, is mighty in power, great in strength: this state of perfection, not formerly attained by this Bhikkhu, is not easily attained; for the sake of which scions of noble family abandon their homes for homelessness and by themselves in this very existence, through the

63

higher knowledge, realize and attain to that supreme consummation, the holy life."

And the Blessed One, in this connection, on that occasion, breathed forth this solemn utterance:

*"The cart rolls on, on one wheel only,*
*But faultless in body, canopied in white:*
*So, see this (miserable dwarf) coming along;*
*He has conquered sorrow, cut off the streams of lust,*
*And freed himself from the bonds (of the desire of future life)."*

6. Thus have I heard. On a certain occasion the Blessed One dwelt at Savatthi, in the Jetavana, the garden of Anâthapindika.

Now at that time the venerable Annâtakondanna was sitting not far from the Blessed One, in a cross-legged position, with body erect contemplating the deliverance that comes through destruction of desire.

And the Blessed One beheld the venerable Annâtakondanna, sitting, not far off, in a cross-legged position, with body erect, contemplating the deliverance that comes from destruction of desire.

And the Blessed One, in this connection, on that occasion, breathed forth this solemn utterance:

*"Where there is neither root, nor earth, nor leaf,*
*How can there be the creeping plant?*
*Who is worthy to reproach the strong man who has escaped from the bonds?*
*Even the gods praise such a one and by Brahma, too, is he extolled."*

7. Thus have I heard. On a certain occasion the Blessed One dwelt at Savatthi, in the Jetavana, the garden of Anâthapindika.

Now at that time the Blessed One was sitting, wrapt in meditation on his own abandonment of consciousness and reasoning in connection with the hindrances.'

And the Blessed One perceiving his own abandonment of consciousness and reasoning, in connection with the hindrances, at that time breathed forth this solemn utterance:

*"He to whom no hindrance remains,*
*Who has overcome all bonds and obstacles*
*Such a saint living free from desire,*
*Nor gods nor men despise."*

8. Thus have I heard. On a certain occasion the Blessed One dwelt at Savatthi, in the Jetavana, the garden of Anâthapindika.

Now at that time the venerable Mahakaccana was sitting, not far from the Blessed One, in a cross-legged position, with body erect, thoroughly setting before him subjective reflection on the impurity of the body.

And the Blessed One beheld the venerable Mahakaccana, sitting near, in a cross-legged position with body erect, thoroughly setting before him subjective reflection on the impurity of the body.

And the Blessed One, in this connection, on that occasion, breathed forth this solemn utterance:

*"He who at all times and continually meditates on the impurity of the body;*
*(It is not, to me it may not be, it will not be, to me it will not be):*
*He, passing on from state to state, in due course,*
*Will cross the poison-streams of desire."*

9. Thus have I heard. At that time the Blessed One, in company with the Brotherhood, was traversing the Malla country and he came to Thuna, a Brahman village, in the Malla country.

And the Brahman housholders of Thuna, on hearing that the Samana Gotama--he who had gone forth from a Sakya family--was traversing the Malla country in company with the Brotherhood and had arrived at Thuna, they filled up the well to the brim with grass and straw, so that these shaven monks, as they called them, should not obtain water to drink.

And the Blessed One, leaving the road, went to the foot of a tree and drawing near sat down on the appointed seat and while thus sitting he said to Ananda: "Bring me, I pray, Ananda, some water from that well."

When these words had been spoken, the venerable Ananda said to the Blessed One: "That well, Sire, has been filled up to the brim with grass and straw by the Brahman housholders of Thuna, so that we, shaven monks, as they call us, may not obtain water to drink."

A second time the Blessed One said to the venerable Ananda: "Bring me, I pray thee, Ananda, some water from that well."

A second time the venerable Ananda said to the Blessed One: 'That well, Sire, has been filled up etc. [as above. *Transl.*].

A third time the Blessed One said to the venerable Ananda: "Bring me, I pray thee, Ananda, some water from that well."

"So be it, Sire" said the venerable Ananda in assent to the Blessed One and he went to the well, taking with him a bowl.

And when he arrived at the well he found that all the grass and straw had been removed and that it was full to the brim, even to overflowing, of pure, clear, translucent water.

And the thought occurred to the venerable Ananda: "How astonishing, how marvellous is the mighty power and great strength of the Perfect One, that on my arrival all the grass and straw were removed and the well was full to the brim, even to overflowing, of clear, pure, translucent water."

And taking some water in the bowl, he went to where the Blessed One was and said to the Blessed One: "How astonishing, how marvellous, is the mighty power and great strength of the Perfect One, by which the grass and straw was removed etc. [as above. *Transl.*].

Drink, Exalted One, of the water: Drink, Happy One, of the water."

And the Blessed One, in this connection, on that occasion, breathed forth this solemn utterance:--

*"When there is water everywhere, what need of a well?*
*When desire has been uprooted,*
*In search of what should a man wander?"*

10. Thus have I heard. On a certain occasion the Blessed One dwelt in the Ghosita garden, at Kosambi.

Now at that time the palace set apart for the royal ladies in the garden of King Udena was burnt down and 500 women perished with Sâmâvati at their head.

And a large number of Bhikkhus robing themselves in the forenoon and taking their alms-bowls and tunics entered Kosambi for alms. And when they had gone their rounds and finished their meal, they went to where the Blessed One was and drawing near they saluted the Blessed One and sat down apart, and while thus sitting they said to the Blessed One: "Just now, Sire, the palace set apart for the royal ladies in the garden of King Udena was burnt down and 500 women perished with Sâmâvati at their head. Whither have these female votaries departed, and what will be their future condition?"

"There are, O Bhikkhus, some lay disciples who have entered the stream, some who return (to this world) once again, some who never return. All these lay disciples who perished are not without reward."

And the Blessed One, in this connection, on that occasion, breathed forth this solemn utterance:--

*"This world of delusions appears good;*
*The fool surrounded by darkness, bound by 'Upadhi',*
*Regards it as eternal.*
*To him who sees aright, it is all nothing."*

# CHAPTER VIII. PATALAGAMI.

1. Thus have I heard. On a certain occasion the Blessed One dwelt at Savatthi, in the Jetavana, the garden of Anâthapindika.

Now at that time the Blessed One was instructing, arousing, animating and gladdening the Bhikkhus with a religious discourse on the subject of Nirvana.

And these Bhikkhus grasping the meaning, thinking it out and accepting with their hearts the whole doctrine, listened attentively.

And the Blessed one, in this connection, on that occasion, breathed forth this solemn utterance:

"There is, O Bhikkhus, a state where there is neither earth, nor water, nor heat nor air, neither infinity of space, nor infinity of consciousness, nor nothingness, nor perception, nor non-perception, neither this world nor that world, both sun und moon.

That, O Bhikkhus, I term neither coming nor going, nor standing, neither death nor birth. It is without stability, without procession, without a basis: that is the end of sorrow".

2. [same as N° 1.] And the Blessed One, in this connection, on that occasion, breathed forth this solemn utterance:

*"Hard is it to realize the essential,*
*The truth is not easily preceived,*
*Desire is mastered by him who knows',*
*To him who sees (aright) all things are naught.*

3. [same as Nᵒˢ 1 and 2.] And the Blessed One, in this connection, on that occasion, breathed forth this solemn utterance:

"There is, O Bhikkhus, an unborn, unoriginated, uncreated, unformed. Were there not, O Bhikkhus, this unborn, unoriginated, uncreated, unformed, there would be no escape from the world of the born, originated, created, formed.

Since, O Bhikkhus, there is an unborn, unoriginated. uncreated, unformed, therefore is there an escape from the born, originated, created, formed".

4. [same as Nᵒˢ 1, 2 and 3] And the Blessed One, in this connection, on that occasion, breathed forth this solemn utterance:

"Where there is dependence, there is instability, where there is no dependence, there is no instability, where there is no instability, there is quietude, where there is quietude, there is no desire, where there is no desire, there is no coming and going, where there is no coming or going, there is no birth or death, where there is no birth or death, there is neither this world nor that world, nor both: that is the end of sorrow".

5. Thus have I heard. At that time the Blessed One in company with the Brotherhood, passing through the Malla country, arrived at Pâvâ.

And the Blessed One tarried at Pâvâ, in the mango grove of Cunda, the potter's son.

And Cunda, the potter's son, heard that the Blessed One, on his way through the Malla country, had arrived at Pâvâ, and was staying in his mango grove.

And Cunda, the potter's son, went to where the Blessed One was and drawing near saluted the Blessed One and sat down apart, and the Blessed One instructed, aroused, animated and gladdened, with religious discourse, Cunda, the potter's son.

And Cunda, the potter's son, instructed, aroused, animated and gladdened by the religious discourse of the Blessed One said: "May it please the Blessed One and the Brotherhood to take their morrow's meal with me".

And the Blessed One assented by his silence.

And Cunda, the potter's son, perceiving that the Blessed One had assented, arose from his seat and saluted the Blessed One, and passing round keeping his right side to him, departed.

And Cunda, the potter's son, at the end of that night having prepared in his own house sweet food, both hard and soft and a quantity of *Sûkaramaddava*, announced to the Blessed One: "Sire, the time is come, the meal is ready."

And the Blessed One, robing himself in the forenoon, and taking his alms-bowl and tunic, went together with the Brotherhood, to the house of Cunda, the potter's son and when he arrived there, sat down on the appointed seat. And while thus seated he called Cunda, the potter's son, to him and said: "The *Sûkaramaddava* you have prepared, Cunda, give to me and the other food, soft and hard, present to the Brethren."

"Be it so, Sire," said Cunda, the potter's son, in assent to the Blessed One, and he gave the *Sûkaramaddava* which he had prepared, to the Blessed One, and the other food, both hard and soft, to the Brethren.

And the Blessed One called Cunda, the potter's son, to him and said: "Bury, Cunda, what remains of the *Sûkaramaddava* in a hole in the ground, for there is no one I know of in the worlds of Mâra or Brahma, or amongst the Samanas or Brahmanas, or in the world of gods and men who can assimilate such food, except the Perfect One."

"Be it so, Sire"; said Cunda, the potter's son, in assent to the Blessed One, and having buried what remained of the *Sûkaramaddava* in a hole, he went to where the Blessed One was and drawing near, he saluted the Blessed One and sat down apart.

And the Blessed One having instructed, aroused, animated and gladdened Cunda, the potter's son, with religious discourse, arose from his seat and departed.

And the Blessed One after partaking of the food provided by Cunda, the potter's son, was seized with a severe malady, and dire pains followed by hemorrhage, even unto death, came upon him.

At that time the Blessed One, ever mindful and intent, endured the pains without a murmur.

And the Blessed One called the venerable Ananda to him and said: "Let us go, Ananda; we will proceed to Kusinâra."

"Be it so, Sire;" said the venerable Ananda in assent to the Blessed One.

"Thus have I heard. He took of the food of Cunda, the the potter's son: With fortitude he bore the grievous, deadly pains: When the master partaok of the Sûkaramaddava, Severe sickness came upon him: After relief, the Blessed One said: 'I will set out for the city of Kusinâra'."

And the Blessed One, leaving the road, went and sat down at the foat of a tree, and calling the venerable Ananda to him, he said: "I pray thee, Ananda, make ready the four-fold cloth, I am weary and would sit down. And the Blessed One sat down on the appointed seat, and thus sitting he called the venerable Ananda to him and said: "I pray thee, Ananda, bring me some water, I am thirsty and would drink, Ananda."

When these words had been spoken the venerable Ananda said to the Blessed One: "Just now, Sire, about 500 wagons have passed over, and the shallow water, disturbed by the wheels, flows turbid and muddy. There is, Sire, not far off, the Kukuttha stream, whose waters are clear, refreshing, cool, pellucid, full to the brim and lovely. There the Blessed One may drink of the waters and cool his limbs."

A second time the Blessed One called the venerable Ananda to him and said: "Bring me, I pray thee, Ananda, some water, I am thirsty and would drink, Ananda."

A second time the venerable Ananda said to the Blessed One: "Just now, Sire, some 500 wagons have passed over, and the shallow water, disturbed by the wheels, flows turbid and muddy. There is, Sire, not far off the Kukuttha stream whose waters are clear, refreshing, cool, pellucid, full to the brim and lovely. There the Blessed One may drink and cool his limbs."

A third time the Blessed One called the venerable Ananda to him and said: "Bring me, Ananda, I pray thee, some water: I am thirsty and would drink, Ananda."

"Be it so, Sire"; said the venerable Ananda in assent to the Blessed One and taking his bowl he went to the river.

And that river, whose shallow waters had been disturbed by the wheels and become a turbid and muddy stream, on the arrival of Ananda, was flowing clear, lucent and untainted.

And Ananda thought: "How strange, how astonishing is the great strength and mighty power of the Perfect One! This stream, whose shallow waters disturbed by the wheels were muddy and polluted, on my arrival, flows pure, lucent and untainted"; and filling his bowl with water he went to where the Blessed One was, and drawing near, said: "How strange, Sire, how astonishing is the great strength and mighty power of the Perfect One! This stream, whose waters etc. [as above] is now pure, lucent and untainted. Drink, O Exalted One, of the water, drink, O Happy One, of the water."

And the Blessed One drank of the water.

And the Blessed One with a great company of the brethren went to the Kukuttha stream, and when he arrived there, he entered the stream and bathed and drank; and when he had come out, he repaired to the Mango-grove and calling the venerable Cundaka to him, said: "I pray thee, Cundaka, spread out for me the four-fold cloth, I am weary, Cundaka, and would lay me down."

"Be it so, Sire"; said the venerable Cundaka in assent to the Blessed One and he spread out the four-fold cloth.

And the Blessed One lay down on his right side, as a lion does, placing one foot upon the other, mindful and consious, and dwelling upon the thought of arising.

And the venerable Cundaka sat there in front of the Exalted One.

"To the pure, joy-giving, pellucid river Kukuttha went the Buddha;

O'erweary, the Master, the Perfect One, the Unequalled in this world, plunged into the stream:

The Master bathed and drank of the waters;

He crossed over preceding the throng of disciples.

The Master, the Exalted One, who set forth the Doctrine, went to the Mango-grove.

He spoke to Cunda, the monk: 'Spread out for me the four-fold cloth.'

Cunda heeded the Holy One, he spread out at once the four-fold cloth.

The Master, the weary One, laid himself down;

And Cunda sat there beside him."

And the Blessed One called the venerable Ananda to him and said: "It may happen, Ananda, that some one may cause Cunda, the potter's son to suffer remorse by saying: 'It is a loss to you, brother Cunda, it is a disadvantage to you, brother Cunda, that the Perfect One should pass away from existence, having received his last meal at you hands.' Any remorse of this kind that may arise in Cunda, the potter's son, should be removed in this wise: 'It is a gain, brother Cunda, it is an advantage to you, brother Cunda, that the Perfect One should pass away from existence, having received his last meal at your hands. Thus have I heard, brother Cunda, in his very presence, these words have I received from the very mouth of the Blessed One: 'there are two alms of the highest profit, of the greatest advantage to me, exceeding all other alms, more fruitful, more replete with resu... What are these two? The alms-food of which the Perfect One partook when ... awakened to supreme enlightenment, and the alms-food of which he partook, w.. ~ he was about to pass away from existence, in that utter passing away in which 'attac.... .' is extinct. These are the two alms, the most perfect in result, the most complet.. their consequence, exceeding all other alms, greater in profit, greater in fruition. The ... able Cunda, the potter's son, has laid up Karma, conducing to length of life, to praise, to heaven, to fame, and to that influence which induces men to follow virtue. Any remorse, Ananda, that may arise in Cunda, the potter's son, should thus be removed'."

And the Blessed One in this connection, on that occasion, breathed forth this solemn utterance:

*"To the giver merit is increased;*
*When the senses are controlled anger arises not.*
*The Wise forsake evil,*
*By the destruction of desire, sin and infatuation,*
*A man attains to Nirvana."*

6. Thus have I heard. At that time the Blessed One, in company with a number of the brethren, wandering through the Magadha country, arrived at Pâtâligâma.

And the lay-disciples of Pâtâligâma heard the report that the Blessed One, in company with a number of the brethren, after wandering through the Magadha county had repaired to Pâtâligâma.

And the lay-disciples of Pâtâligâma went to where the Blessed One was and drawing near they saluted the Blessed One and sat down apart, and while thus sitting the lay-disciples of Pâtâligâma said to the Blessed One: "May it please the Blessed One to come to our house."

And the Blessed One assented by his silence.

And the lay-disciples of Pâtâligâma perceiving that the Blessed One had assented, they arose from their seats and saluted the Blessed One, and passing round with their right sides to him, they returned to their rest-house. And when they arrived there, they set the house in order, arranging the seats, providing water vessels, and putting up oil-lamps. And when they had done this, they went to where the Blessed One was and drawing near, they saluted the Blessed One and stood respectfully apart, and while thus standing the lay-disciples of Pâtâligâma said to the Blessed One: "Sire, the rest-house is set in order, the seats are arranged, the water vessels provided and the oil-lamps put up. May the Blessed One now do as he pleases."

And the Blessed One, robing himself in the forenoon and taking his alms-bowl and tunic, went, together with the Brethren, to the rest-house. And when the Blessed One arrived there, having washed his feet, he entered the rest-house and sat down near the centre pillar, facing the East, and the Brethren, also, having washed their feet, entered the rest-house and sat down near the centre wall, facing the East, the Blessed One being in front of them; and the lay-disciples of Pâtâligâma, having washed their feet, entered the rest-house and sat down near the Eastern wall with their faces to the West, the Blessed One in front of them.

And the Blessed One thus addressed the lay-disciples of Pâtâligâma:

"Five losses, O housholders, result to the wrong door through his want of rectitude. What are these five?

(1) In this world, O housholders, the wrong-doer failing in rectitude, in consequence of sloth, suffers great loss of property. This is the first loss to the wrong-doer through want of rectitude.

(2) Further, O housholders, in the case of the wrong-doer, who fails in virtue, an evil repute arises. This is the second loss to the wrong-doer who fails in virtue.

(3) Further, O housholders, whenever a wrong-doer, failing in virtue, approaches assemblies, whether of Khattiyas, or Brahmanas, or lay men, or Samanas, he feels ashamed and troubled in their presence. This is the third loss to a wrong-doer who fails in virtue.

(4) Further, O housholders, the wrong-doer who fails in virtue, dies in a state of unrest. This is the fourth loss to a wrong-doer who fails in virtue.

(5) Further, O housholders, the wrong-doer, wanting in rectitude, on the dissolution of the body, after death, is born into a state of punishment, of suffering, of torment, in hell. This is the fifth loss to a wrong-doer through want of rectitude.

These, O housholders, are the five losses to the wrong-doer, through want of rectitude.

There are five gains, O housholders, to the virtuous man, through the practise of virtue. What are these five?

(1) In this world, O housholders, the upright man who practises virtue, by means of diligence acquires abundant possessions. This is the first gain to an upright man who practises virtue.

(2) Further, O housholders, in the case of an upright man who practises virtue, there arises a fair repute. This is the second gain to an upright man who practises virtue.

(3) Further, O housholders, whenever an upright man who practises virtue, approaches assemblies whether of Khattiyas, or Brahmanas, or laymen, or Samanas, he is not ashamed or troubled when he approaches them. This is the third gain to the upright man who practises virtue.

(4) Further, O housholders, the upright man who practises virtue, dies peacefully. This is the fourth gain to an upright man, who practises virtue.

(5) Further, O housholders, the upright man who practises virtue, on the dissolution of the body after death, is born into a state of happiness, in

heaven. This is the fifth gain to an upright man who practises virtue. These, O housholders, are the five gains to the upright man who practises virtue."

And the Blessed One having instructed, aroused, animated and gladdened the lay-disciples with this religious discourse, dismissed them, saying: "The night, O housholders, is far spent. Do now as seemeth fit to you."

And the lay-disciples of Pâtâligâma, having praised the words of the Blessed One, and given thanks, arose from their seats, and passing round keeping their right sides to him, took their departure.

And the Blessed One, soon after the departure of the lay-disciples of Pâtâligâma, entered his private apartments.

Now at that time the Sunîdhavassakâras, the ministers of Magadha, had built a fortress at Pâtâligâma, to repel the Vajjis. And at that time also, a great number, some thousands of Devas, haunted the dwellings at Pâtâligâma. Wherever the most powerful Devas haunted the houses, in that place they induced the most powerful kings and king's ministers to build dwelling places. Wherever the lesser Devas haunted the houses, there they induced the lesser kings and king's ministers to build dwelling places, and wherever the lowest Devas haunted the houses, there they induced the lowest kings and king's Ministers to build dwelling places.

And the Blessed One, with his divine, clear sight, surpassing that of men, beheld these thousands of Devas who haunted the houses at Pâtâligâma, and wherever the most powerful Devas, etc. [as above. *Transl.*]

And the Blessed One, in the dawn following that night, called the venerable Ananda to him and said: "Who, Ananda, built this fortress at Pâtâligâma"?

"The Sunîdhavassakâras, the ministers of Magadha, built this fortress at Pâtâligâma, to repel the Vajjis."

"It seems, Ananda, as if the Sunîdhavassakâras, the Ministers of Magadha, after consulting with the Tavatimsa gods, had thus, Ananda, built this fortress at Pâtâligâma, to repel the Vajjis. I have just seen, Ananda, with my divine and clear sight, surpassing that of men, this large number of thousands of Devas who haunt the houses at Pâtâligâma. Wherever the most powerful Devas etc. [as above. *Transl.*].

Wherever, Ananda, famous places, centres of trade may be, this fortified city will be chief among them, an emporium of commerce. But, Ananda, three disasters will befall Pâtâligâma, by fire and water and internal dissensions."

And the Sunîdhivassakâras, the ministers of Magadha went to where the Blessed One was and drawing near they exchanged friendly greetings with the Blessed One, and when they had exchanged with him the compliments of friendship and civility, they stationed themselves respectfully apart, and while thus standing the Sunîdhavassakâras, the ministers of Magadha said to the Blessed One: "May it please the Lord Gotama, and the Brethren to take their meal with us to-day."

The Blessed One assented by his silence.

And the Sunîdhavassakâras, the ministers of Mâgadha, perceiving that the Blessed One had assented, went to their own house, and when they arrived there, gave orders for the preparation of sweet food, both hard and soft, and they announced to the Blessed One, that the time had come; "Lord Gotama, the time is come, the meal is ready."

And the Blessed One, robing himself in the forenoon and taking his alms-bowl and tunic, went, in company with the Brethren, to the house of the Sunîdhavassakâras; and when they arrived there, they sat down on the appointed seats.

And the Sunîdhivassakâras, with their own hands, served and offered sweet food, both hard and soft, to the Brethren with the Buddha at their head.

And when the Blessed One had withdrawn his hand from the bowl and finished his meal, the Sunîdhivassakâras having taken a lower place, sat dov ι apart, and the Blessed One, as they sat thus, gladdened the Su .dhivassakâras with these verses:

"In whatever country, the wise man dwells,
Maintaining the virtuous, the self-controlled, the holy ones,
Let him present offerings to the Devas who are there,
And they so honoured and venerated, will honour and venerate him,
And hereafter show compassion, as a mother to her son.
He who receives the compassion of the Devas, never lacks good fortune."

And the Blessed One, when he had gladdened the Sunîdhavassakâras with these verses, arose from his seat and departed.

Now at that time the Sunîdhivassakâras followed the Blessed One, step by step, saying: "The gate by which the Samana Gotama this day departs, shall be called the Gotama gate, the ford by which he crosses the Ganga river, shall be called the Gotama ford.

And the gate, by which the Blessed One passed out was called the Gotama gate.

And the Blessed One came to where the river Ganga was. Now at that time, the river was full, up to the bank, so that a crow could have drunk from it. Some men, eager to cross, were in search of a boat, some in search of a raft, others were engaged in constructing a raft.

And the Blessed One, just as if a strong man should out-stretch his bent arm or bend back his out-stretched arm, even so he vanished from the hither bank of the river Ganga and stood upon the opposite bank with the Brethren.

And the Blessed One beheld those men, eager to cross, some in search of a boat, some in search of a raft, and others engaged in constructing a raft.

And the Blessed One, in this connection, on that occasion, breathed forth this solemn utterance:

*"Those who cross the ocean, having built a bridge, forsaking the marshes--*
*While the world is constructing rafts--these wise ones escape."*

7. Thus have I heard. At that time the Blessed One had reached the high road in the Kosala country, with the venerable Nâgasamâla as attendant.

And the venerable Nâgasamâla observed on the way that the road diverged, and seeing this, he said to the Blessed One; "Sire, this is the way, let us go in this direction."

When these words had been spoken, the Blessed One said to the venerable Nâgasamâla: "This is the way, Nâgasamâla, let us go in this direction."

[Repetition of speech and reply. *Transl.*].

A third time the venerable Nâgasamâla said to the Blessed One: "This, Sire, is the way, let us go in this direction." And the venerable Nâgasamâla threw down on the ground the bowl and tunic of the Blessed One, saying: "There, Sire, are your bowl and tunic."

And as the venerable Nâgasamâla proceeded on the road, robbers came and assaulted him with their hands and feet, broke his alms-bowl and tore his garments. And the venerable Nâgasamâla, with broken bowl and torn garments went to where the Blessed One was, and drawing near he saluted the Blessed One and sat down respectfully apart and while thus sitting he said to the Blessed One: "Just now, Sire, as I was proceeding on the road, robbers came and assaulted me with their hands and feet, broke my alms-bowl and tore my garments."

And the Blessed One, in this connection, on that occasion, breathed forth this solemn utterance:--

*"He who walks with another, lives with him, associates with him,*
*He, the learned One, perceiving evil, forsakes it,*
*As the young heron abandons the river."*

8. Thus have I heard. On a certain occasion the Blessed One dwelt at Savatthi, in the Eastern monastery, in the pavilion of Visâkha-migâramâta.

Now at that time, the dearly loved grandson of Visâkha-migâramâta died.

And Visâkha-migâramâta went at unseasonable hours, with hands and hair wet (with tears), to where the Blessed One was and drawing near she saluted the Blessed One and sat down apart. And the Blessed One said to Visâkha-migâramâta, as he sat there: Wherefore, O Visâkha, do you come here at unseasonable hours, with hands and hair wet (with tears)?"

"Sire, my dearly loved grandson is dead; that is why I come here, at unseasonable hours, with hands and hair wet (with tears)."

"Do you find, O Visâkha, that there are sons and grandsons in proportion to the number of men in Savatthi?"

"I find, Blessed One, that there are sons and grandsons in proportion to the number of men."

"And how many men of Savatthi, Visâkha, die daily?"

"Sometimes, Sire, ten men of Savatthi die daily, sometimes nine, eight, seven, six, five, four, three, two; sometimes, Sire, only one man dies in the day. Of men dying in Savatthi, there is no lack, Sire."

"What think you, Visâkha; have you found at any time or anywhere, men whose garments have been unwetted (by tears), whose hair has been unwetted (by tears)?"

"Not so, Sire; how is that possible with so many sons and grandsons?"

"Those, Visâkha, who have a hundred dear ones, have a hundred sorrows, these who have ninety dear ones, have ninety sorrows, these who have eighty dear ones, have eighty sorrows etc. those who have one dear one, have one sorrow.

Those who have no dear one, for them there is no sorrow.

These, I declare, are the griefless ones, free from human passion, without despair.

*"Whatsoever of sorrow, lamentation and pain is in the world,*
*All this arises from clinging, where clinging is not, these are not.*
*Therefore happy and sorrowless are those who cling not to any thing in the world.*
*Set not your affections on things on earth."*

9. Thus have I heard. On a certain occasion the Blessed One dwelt at Râjagaha, in the Bamboo-grove, in Kalandakanivâpa.

And the venerable Dubba Mallaputta went to where the Blessed One was and drawing near he saluted the Blessed One and sat down respectfully apart, and while thus sitting he said to the Blessed One: "The time, O Happy One, for my passing away from existence has come."

"Do, O Dubba, as seemeth right."

And the venerable Dubba Mallaputta, got up from his seat and saluted the Blessed One and having passed round keeping his right side to him, he rose into the air, sitting cross-legged in the firmament, and when he had attained to that state of mystic meditation induced by fixed attention on one predominant idea (in this case that of fire), he rose still higher and finally passed into Nirvana.

And when the venerable Dubba Mallaputta had thus risen into the air; sitting cross-legged in the firmament, and attaining to that state of mystic meditation induced by fixed attention on one predominant idea (in this case, that of fire) and rising still higher passed into Nirvana, of his body which was burnt and consumed by flames, there was no residue either of ashes or soot to be seen.

As in the case of butter or oil when they are burnt and consumed by flames, there is no residue either of ashes or soot, so was it with the venerable Dubba Mallaputta, when his body was burnt and consumed by fire, there was no residue of ashes or soot to be seen, after he had risen into the air and sat cross-legged in the firmament, having attained to that state of mystic meditation induced by fixed attention on one predominant idea (that of fire) and when arising still higher passed into Nirvana.

And the Blessed One, in this connection, on that occasion, breathed forth this solemn utterance:

*"The body is dissolved, perception annihilated, all sensations have ceased,*
*The elements of being are extinguished, Consciousness has sunk to rest."*

10. Thus have I heard. On a certain occasion the Blessed One dwelt at Savatthi, in the Jetavana, the garden of Anâthapindika.

And the Blessed One called his disciples to him and said: "O Disciples."

"Sire", said those disciples in attention to the Blessed One.

And the Blessed One said: "When Dubba Mallaputta, O disciples, rose into the air and sat cross-legged in the firmament there was no residue etc. [as above. *Transl.*].

And the Blessed One, in this connection, on that occasion, breathed forth this solemn utterance:

*"As the fiery sparks from a forge, one by one, are extinguished*
*And no one knows whither they have gone;*
*So is it with those who have attained to complete emancipation,*
*Who have crossed the flood of desire.*
*Who have entered upon the tranquil joy (of Nirvana)--*
*Of these no trace remains."*

www.ingramcontent.com/pod-product-compliance
Lightning Source LLC
Chambersburg PA
CBHW071926020426
42331CB00010B/2745